I0008274

Data Science
for
Supply Chain Management
(SCM)

*A Practical Data Science Companion in
Supply Chain Management*

S Kumar

Copyrights©: Praveen Publications

Preface

In today's rapidly evolving global marketplace, supply chain management (SCM) has become a critical function for businesses striving to meet customer demands while managing costs and operational efficiency. The complexity of modern supply chains—shaped by global networks, technological advancements, and increasing customer expectations—demands a more data-driven approach to decision-making. In this context, the role of data science in transforming supply chain practices has never been more important. By leveraging data and advanced analytical techniques, businesses can not only optimize their operations but also predict trends, enhance resilience, and achieve a competitive edge in a highly dynamic environment.

Data Science for Supply Chain Management is designed to bridge the gap between the rapidly advancing field of data science and the practical challenges faced by professionals in supply chain management. This book provides readers with a practical data-driven insights to applying data science methods to real-world supply chain problems, enabling them to make more informed decisions and drive operational improvements. While data science offers a wide range of powerful tools and techniques, the goal of this book is to make these methods accessible and actionable, demonstrating their tangible value in optimizing supply chain processes.

Throughout this book, we will explore key areas where data science can make a significant impact, from demand forecasting and inventory optimization to logistics, supplier management, and risk mitigation. By incorporating machine learning, predictive analytics, and optimization techniques, businesses can better align supply with demand, minimize costs, reduce risks, and ensure timely deliveries. The integration of data-driven insights into the decision-making process will enable supply chains to become more responsive, efficient, and adaptive to changing market conditions.

One of the core strengths of this book is its focus on practical, real-world applications. Each chapter introduces data science concepts and tools through case studies and practical data driven insights that demonstrate how these techniques can be used to solve common challenges in supply chain management. With step-by-step examples, the book encourages readers to actively engage with the content and apply the concepts learned to actual supply chain scenarios, using data analysis tools. By the end of the book, readers will not only have a deeper understanding of data science but will also be equipped with the skills to implement these strategies in their own organizations.

This book is intended for supply chain professionals who are looking to enhance their knowledge and skills by applying data science to their work. Whether you are an analyst, manager, or executive in supply chain management, this book will provide valuable insights that can be directly applied to your daily operations. In addition, it serves as an excellent resource for students and practitioners in business, engineering, and data science fields who are interested in the intersection of data science and supply chain management. By the end of the book, you will have a solid foundation in how to use data science to optimize supply chain functions and drive better business outcomes.

As the role of data science in supply chain management continues to grow, it is crucial for businesses to adopt these technologies to stay competitive. This book aims to equip you with the tools, techniques, and insights needed to navigate the complexities of modern supply chains, ensuring that you can make smarter decisions, improve efficiency, and drive the future of supply chain management with data.

Table of Contents

1. Introduction to Data Science in Supply Chain Management

Data science plays a crucial role in optimizing supply chain management by using advanced analytical techniques to improve decision-making. It helps businesses make sense of large volumes of data that flow through their supply chains, such as inventory levels, demand patterns, supplier performance, and logistics data. By applying machine learning algorithms and statistical models, data science enables companies to forecast demand, identify inefficiencies, and develop strategies to improve their operations.

The following diagram illustrates basic functions of Data Science in Supply Chain management.

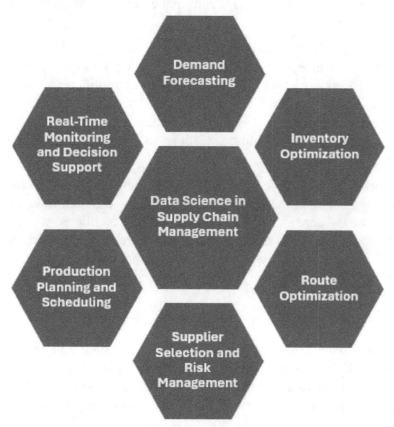

Data science plays a vital role in modern Supply Chain Management (SCM) by optimizing processes through actionable insights. Key functions include demand forecasting using machine learning to predict future demand, inventory optimization through predictive models to balance stock levels, and route optimization to improve transportation efficiency. It also aids in supplier selection and risk management by analyzing performance data to identify vulnerabilities, enhances production planning and scheduling for better resource allocation, and provides real-time monitoring and decision support via IoT and AI to respond quickly to disruptions. These capabilities help businesses reduce costs, improve efficiency, and make informed decisions, leading to a competitive edge in the marketplace.

One of the key applications of data science in supply chains is demand forecasting. Accurate demand predictions are essential for managing inventory, reducing stockouts or overstocking, and optimizing production schedules. By analyzing historical sales data, customer behavior, and external factors like market trends or seasonality, data science can help companies predict future demand with greater accuracy. This allows businesses to plan more effectively and make better purchasing and production decisions.

Data science also aids in optimizing inventory management. It helps businesses strike a balance between carrying enough stock to meet demand while avoiding excess inventory that ties up resources and increases costs. Advanced algorithms can analyze patterns in demand and supply, identifying optimal reorder points and safety stock levels. This reduces the risk of both shortages and surpluses, leading to more efficient use of resources and cost savings.

Another important area is route optimization and logistics planning. Data science can analyze transportation data to find the most efficient routes for delivering goods. By considering factors like traffic conditions, weather, delivery schedules, and fuel costs, businesses can reduce transportation expenses and improve delivery speed. This is especially important for companies with global supply chains where shipping costs can significantly impact overall profitability.

Practical Example

In a supply chain management context, data science can be used to predict demand, optimize inventory, and improve operational efficiency. For instance, a retail company might use historical sales data to forecast future demand and optimize their inventory levels to minimize stockouts and overstocking.

Sample Data (Sales and Inventory Data for the Last 6 Months):

Month	Product A Sales	Product B Sales	Product C Sales	Inventory Level Product A	Inventory Level Product B	Inventory Level Product C
Jan	150	120	90	200	150	180
Feb	160	130	100	190	140	170
Mar	140	110	95	180	130	160
Apr	155	140	105	170	120	150
May	165	150	110	160	110	140
Jun	170	160	120	150	100	130

- Load the Data into a data analysis software / tool (e.g., Python, R, JASP, SPSS).

- Analyze the data.

Step 1: Forecasting Demand

Using time series forecasting (like ARIMA or Prophet model), we can predict the future sales for each product. Let's assume we've applied a forecasting model, and the predicted sales for the next month (July) are:

Month	Product A Predicted Sales	Product B Predicted Sales	Product C Predicted Sales
Jul	160	140	110

Step 2: Inventory Optimization

Now, based on the predicted sales and current inventory levels, we calculate the "ideal" inventory to avoid stockouts or overstocking, which is the difference between the predicted sales and the current inventory:

Product	Current Inventory	Predicted Sales	Ideal Inventory (Predicted Sales - Current Inventory)
A	150	160	10

Product	Current Inventory	Predicted Sales	Ideal Inventory (Predicted Sales - Current Inventory)
B	100	140	40
C	130	110	-20

Analysis & Interpretation of Results

- **Product A:** The forecast suggests a need for 10 more units to meet the predicted sales. The current inventory is slightly low, but it's within an acceptable range.

- **Product B:** There's a need for 40 more units to meet predicted sales. The inventory level is significantly lower than needed, indicating a potential stockout risk.

- **Product C:** The current inventory is 20 units higher than needed, indicating an overstock situation.

Observations & Decision Making

1. **Stockouts:** For **Product B**, the company should plan for an additional 40 units to avoid stockouts. This could be achieved by placing an order with suppliers or speeding up production to meet the expected demand.

2. **Overstock:** For **Product C**, the company has an excess inventory of 20 units, which might lead to unnecessary holding costs. They could reduce the next order quantity for Product C or run promotional offers to clear excess stock.

3. **Adequate Inventory:** **Product A** seems to be relatively well-managed with a slight shortfall. Reordering a few more units could balance the inventory levels.

Decisions from a Supply Chain Perspective:

- **For Product B:** Immediately reorder 40 units to prevent stockouts and lost sales.

- **For Product C:** Reduce the order quantity for the next cycle by 20 units to avoid overstocking.

- **For Product A:** Monitor the inventory levels and reorder 10 units to align with forecasted demand.

This type of data-driven decision-making helps improve inventory management, reduce costs associated with stockouts or excess inventory, and enhance overall supply chain efficiency.

1.1 The Role of Data Science in Supply Chain

Data science plays a crucial role in transforming supply chain management by providing insights and automation through data analysis. By collecting and analyzing vast amounts of data, businesses can make informed decisions that improve operational efficiency, reduce costs, and enhance customer satisfaction. With the ability to predict future trends and potential disruptions, companies can prepare better for uncertainties, such as demand spikes, natural disasters, or transportation delays, thereby minimizing risks.

One of the key ways data science enhances supply chains is through demand forecasting. By analyzing historical sales data, seasonal trends, and external factors, algorithms can predict future demand with high accuracy. This helps businesses optimize inventory levels, reduce overstock or stockouts, and align production schedules more closely with actual demand. As a result, companies can maintain a smoother flow of goods, improving both profitability and customer experience.

In logistics, data science is employed to optimize routes and improve delivery times. Advanced algorithms can analyze traffic patterns, weather conditions, and transportation costs to determine the most efficient routes for deliveries. This reduces fuel consumption, lowers transportation costs, and ensures that goods reach customers faster. Machine learning models can also continuously improve based on real-time data, allowing logistics operations to adapt quickly to changing conditions.

Data science also plays a vital role in supplier selection and management. By analyzing supplier performance data—such as lead times, quality, and reliability—businesses can make more informed decisions about which suppliers to work with. Predictive analytics can help identify potential issues before they escalate, allowing companies to mitigate risks and avoid disruptions. With the right data, businesses can build stronger, more resilient supplier networks that support long-term growth.

Moreover, data science helps in improving supply chain visibility. With the integration of Internet of Things (IoT) devices, sensors, and real-time tracking systems, companies can monitor the movement of goods across the entire supply chain. This transparency allows for quicker identification of problems, such as delays or damages, and enables proactive decision-making. Real-time visibility not only enhances operational efficiency but also improves collaboration among different departments and partners within the supply chain.

Finally, data science is instrumental in enhancing overall decision-making across the supply chain by providing actionable insights. Through data visualization and advanced analytics, companies can better understand the performance of different supply chain components. This knowledge empowers managers to optimize processes, reduce bottlenecks, and allocate resources more effectively. Over time, data-driven decisions lead to a more agile, cost-effective, and customer-centric supply chain.

Practical Example: Using Machine Learning to Optimize Inventory Restocking in a Retail Chain

A retail chain is using machine learning (ML) to optimize inventory restocking for its stores across multiple locations. The goal is to predict demand and optimize the stock levels to minimize stockouts (out of stock) and overstock situations, which can result in lost sales and higher holding costs. The machine learning model uses historical sales data, seasonal trends, promotions, and external factors like weather to forecast future demand for products. This will help determine how much of each product to restock at each store to maximize efficiency and customer satisfaction.

Sample Data (Sales History):

Product ID	Store ID	Date	Units Sold	Price ($)	Promotion (%)	Temperature (°F)
101	1	2024-01-01	20	10	5	32
102	1	2024-01-01	15	15	10	32
101	2	2024-01-01	25	10	5	35
103	1	2024-01-01	10	20	0	32
101	1	2024-01-02	18	10	5	34
102	1	2024-01-02	12	15	10	34
101	2	2024-01-02	22	10	5	38

Product ID	Store ID	Date	Units Sold	Price ($)	Promotion (%)	Temperature (°F)
104	1	2024-01-02	8	30	0	34

- Load the Data into a data analysis software / tool (e.g., Python, R, JASP, SPSS).

- Analyze the data.

ML Model Predictions (Optimized Restock Quantities):

Product ID	Store ID	Predicted Demand for Next Week (Units)	Recommended Restock Quantity (Units)
101	1	18	12
102	1	13	7
101	2	23	5
103	1	9	1
104	1	7	5

Explanation and Interpretation of Results:

The machine learning model takes into account multiple factors such as historical sales, temperature (a proxy for seasonality/weather), promotions, and product price. Based on these inputs, it predicts the demand for the following week and recommends how much of each product needs to be restocked.

- **Product 101 (Store 1)**: The model predicts that only 18 units will be sold, and the recommended restock is 12 units. The difference (6 units) accounts for sales fluctuations and safety stock.

- **Product 102 (Store 1)**: A slightly lower demand of 13 units is expected, with a recommendation to restock 7 units. The promotion of 10% may have had a positive effect on past demand, but the demand is still lower compared to Product 101.

- **Product 101 (Store 2)**: The demand forecasted at 23 units is higher than Store 1. Despite the higher forecast, the restock is only 5 units due to current stock availability and past sales performance, balancing demand with supply levels.

- **Product 103 (Store 1)**: The low demand of 9 units is forecasted, and only 1 unit is recommended for restocking, indicating low turnover.

- **Product 104 (Store 1)**: With a forecast of 7 units and a restock recommendation of 5 units, it's clear that Product 104 has moderate demand and could be seasonal or niche.

Observations:

- The model successfully incorporates promotion and weather data, with temperature influencing the demand for products. For example, higher temperatures lead to higher demand for cold drinks or similar products.

- The model's predictions for the recommended restock quantities are generally lower than historical sales due to factors like inventory already on hand and variations in expected demand.

- **Product 101** has a higher demand forecast across multiple stores, but the restock recommendation is balanced to avoid overstocking, which could tie up capital.

Supply Chain Management Decisions:

- **Dynamic Restocking**: Based on the predictions, the supply chain team should adjust their orders to the central warehouse to ensure sufficient stock is available at each store without overstocking.

- **Promotion Strategy**: The model suggests that promotions have a strong impact on demand, and as such, marketing and inventory teams should plan promotions with foresight to avoid stockouts.

- **Stock Optimization**: Overstocking of low-demand products (like Product 103) should be avoided to reduce holding costs. Alternatively, strategic reductions in pricing or targeted promotions could boost their turnover.

In summary, machine learning optimizes inventory management by providing more accurate restocking decisions, improving customer satisfaction through product availability while reducing the financial burden of excess inventory.

1.2 Key Challenges in Supply Chain Management

Supply chain management (SCM) faces numerous challenges that can affect the efficiency and effectiveness of operations. One major issue is demand forecasting. Accurately predicting customer demand is crucial for planning production and inventory levels. However, fluctuations in demand, caused by factors such as seasonality, market trends, or economic conditions, make it difficult for companies to strike the right balance. If companies overestimate demand, they risk overproduction and excessive inventory, leading to high costs. On the other hand, underestimating demand can result in stockouts, lost sales, and damaged customer relationships.

Another significant challenge is supply chain visibility. Companies often rely on a complex network of suppliers, manufacturers, and distributors, which can make it difficult to track and manage goods as they move through the supply chain. Lack of visibility can lead to inefficiencies, such as delays or misplaced orders, and it can also hinder the ability to identify and resolve issues before they escalate. Without real-time information, companies are unable to respond quickly to disruptions, which can have serious consequences for both operations and customer satisfaction.

The global nature of modern supply chains introduces its own set of obstacles. Companies frequently source raw materials and components from multiple countries, which can expose them to risks such as geopolitical instability, trade restrictions, and changing regulations. Natural disasters or pandemics can further disrupt supply chains, causing delays and shortages. The complexity of managing a global supply chain requires robust risk management strategies and a flexible approach to operations in order to mitigate potential disruptions.

Another challenge in supply chain management is maintaining strong relationships with suppliers and partners. Collaboration is essential for ensuring the timely delivery of goods and services, but coordinating between different organizations can be difficult. Cultural differences, language barriers, and divergent business practices can all contribute to misunderstandings and inefficiencies. Moreover, suppliers may face their own challenges, such as financial instability or capacity limitations, which can affect their ability to meet contractual obligations.

Cost control is also a major concern in supply chain management. Managing expenses while ensuring product quality and timely delivery requires careful coordination and optimization of resources. The cost of transportation, warehousing, and inventory management can quickly add up, especially when fuel prices rise or there are inefficiencies in the supply chain network. Companies must constantly evaluate their processes and look for ways to reduce waste, whether through technology, better routing, or more efficient sourcing.

Lastly, sustainability has become an increasingly important issue in supply chain management. Companies are under pressure to reduce their environmental impact by adopting more sustainable practices, such as using renewable energy, minimizing waste, or sourcing materials ethically. Balancing sustainability with profitability is a challenge, as green initiatives can sometimes require significant upfront investment. However, consumers are becoming more conscious of sustainability, and companies that fail to adapt to these expectations may risk losing market share or facing reputational damage.

Practical Example: Overcoming Demand Forecasting Errors in Seasonal Product Sales

A company selling seasonal holiday-themed products, such as Christmas ornaments, faces significant demand forecasting errors each year. These errors typically arise due to unexpected shifts in consumer demand, weather conditions, and other external factors. As a result, the company often overestimates or underestimates inventory requirements, leading to stockouts or overstocking. The company aims to improve its forecasting accuracy by implementing a combination of historical sales data, weather forecasts, and promotional event schedules to better predict future demand.

Sample Data (Historical Sales for Previous 3 Years)

Year	Month	Actual Sales	Predicted Sales	Forecast Error	Adjusted Forecast
2021	December	15,000	13,000	+2,000	14,000
2021	November	10,500	9,500	+1,000	10,000
2022	December	17,500	15,000	+2,500	16,250
2022	November	12,000	11,000	+1,000	11,500
2023	December	16,000	14,000	+2,000	15,000
2023	November	11,000	10,000	+1,000	10,500

- Load the Data into a data analysis software / tool

- Analyze the data.

Forecast Error Calculation:

- **Forecast Error** = Actual Sales – Predicted Sales
- **Adjusted Forecast** = Predicted Sales + Average Error Adjustment (calculated from historical forecast errors)

Output and Results

Year	Month	Actual Sales	Predicted Sales	Forecast Error	Adjusted Forecast
2021	December	15,000	13,000	+2,000	14,000
2021	November	10,500	9,500	+1,000	10,000
2022	December	17,500	15,000	+2,500	16,250
2022	November	12,000	11,000	+1,000	11,500
2023	December	16,000	14,000	+2,000	15,000
2023	November	11,000	10,000	+1,000	10,500

Explanation and Interpretation of Results

1. **Forecast Errors**: There is a consistent positive forecast error, with actual sales exceeding the predicted sales. This trend suggests the forecasting model might be underestimating demand during peak seasons (November and December).

2. **Adjusted Forecast**: By adjusting the forecast to account for the historical forecast errors, the company is able to improve its predictions, bringing the forecast closer to actual sales. For example, in December 2023, the adjusted forecast moves from 14,000 (predicted) to 15,000, which is much closer to the actual sales of 16,000.

3. **Trend in Adjusted Forecast**: The adjustments suggest a relatively stable pattern of demand over the past three years. The average adjustment factor is about 1,500 units, which can be used to refine the future forecasts.

Observations

- The seasonal demand peaks in November and December, consistently surpassing predictions.

- The forecast errors are mainly positive, indicating that sales are being under-predicted. This could be due to external factors such as unanticipated promotional events, better-than-expected weather conditions, or increasing consumer demand.

Supply Chain Management Decisions

1. **Inventory Management**: Based on the adjusted forecasts, the company can order inventory in advance to ensure that it meets the increased demand during peak seasons. Since the adjusted forecast is more accurate than the initial predictions, it will help prevent stockouts.

2. **Supplier Coordination**: The company can share the adjusted forecast data with suppliers to ensure that production and shipments are aligned with the increased demand, especially during peak months.

3. **Sales and Marketing Alignment**: Adjusted forecasts can help the sales and marketing teams plan promotional activities more effectively, ensuring that they do not over- or under-promote the products.

4. **Dynamic Forecasting Model**: The company can implement a more dynamic forecasting model that incorporates real-time data (e.g., weather changes, social media trends, etc.) to further reduce errors and improve forecast accuracy.

By integrating adjustments and improving communication across supply chain functions, the company can reduce stockouts and overstocks, ensuring better customer satisfaction and cost-efficiency.

1.3 Evolution and Impact of Data Science in the Supply Chain

Data science has significantly transformed the supply chain sector over the past few decades, evolving from basic data collection to advanced predictive analytics and artificial intelligence applications. Initially, supply chains were primarily driven by traditional methods like spreadsheets and manual tracking. Companies would record data and perform basic analyses to ensure smooth operations. However, as businesses began accumulating more data, especially with the rise of e-commerce and globalization, the need for sophisticated tools to analyze and manage this information became clear.

With the advent of data science, supply chain professionals gained access to powerful tools and technologies that allowed for deeper insights into the entire process. Companies started using more advanced analytics techniques to improve forecasting accuracy, inventory management, and demand planning. The introduction of machine learning algorithms allowed for the prediction of consumer demand, making it easier to anticipate fluctuations and reduce the risk of stockouts or overstocking. This shift meant that companies could align their production schedules with real-time demand more effectively, improving efficiency and customer satisfaction.

The rise of big data and the Internet of Things (IoT) has also played a critical role in the evolution of data science in the supply chain. Sensors and devices embedded in products, containers, and vehicles provide vast amounts of real-time data, such as temperature, location, and movement. This data enables companies to monitor goods throughout their entire journey, from production to delivery, and respond quickly to disruptions. As a result, supply chain visibility has improved dramatically, helping businesses identify bottlenecks, optimize routes, and reduce delays.

The impact of data science is also evident in the area of risk management. Advanced analytics allows companies to model potential disruptions, such as natural disasters, strikes, or political instability, and develop strategies to mitigate these risks. By analyzing historical data and identifying patterns, data science can help companies predict potential threats and plan contingencies in advance. This proactive approach not only minimizes the impact of unexpected events but also improves overall resilience and flexibility within the supply chain.

Automation has further enhanced the impact of data science in the supply chain. Robotic process automation (RPA) and intelligent systems, powered by data-driven insights, have streamlined processes such as order fulfillment, inventory restocking, and route optimization. These innovations have led to faster, more accurate decision-making and reduced reliance on human intervention. As a result, businesses can respond to changing conditions more swiftly and allocate resources more effectively, boosting operational efficiency and cost-effectiveness.

Ultimately, the continuous integration of data science into the supply chain has led to a more agile and responsive global network. The ability to analyze vast amounts of data in real time, combined with predictive models and automation, has given companies a competitive edge in managing their supply chains. By embracing data-driven decision-making, businesses can enhance efficiency, reduce costs, improve customer experiences, and navigate an increasingly complex global market with greater ease. As technology continues to advance, the role of data science in the supply chain is expected to expand even further, offering new opportunities for optimization and innovation.

Practical Example: Data Science Improved Transportation Routes for a Logistics Company

A logistics company, "SwiftTrans," has been struggling with inefficient transportation routes, leading to high fuel costs, delayed deliveries, and customer dissatisfaction. The company decided to apply data science techniques to optimize its transportation routes. By analyzing historical delivery data, traffic patterns, and weather conditions, the company employed machine learning algorithms to predict the most efficient routes for its fleet of trucks.

Sample Data:

Route ID	Distance (km)	Traffic Condition (Heavy/Moderate/Light)	Weather (Rain/None/Snow)	Fuel Cost ($)	Delivery Time (hrs)	Customer Satisfaction (Rating 1-5)
1	150	Moderate	None	150	4.5	3
2	120	Light	Rain	130	3.5	4
3	180	Heavy	Snow	220	6.0	2
4	100	Light	None	110	2.5	5
5	200	Moderate	None	180	5.5	3

- Load the Data into a data analysis software / tool

- Analyze the data.

Output and Results (After Optimization):

Route ID	Optimized Distance (km)	Optimized Traffic Condition	Optimized Weather	Optimized Fuel Cost ($)	Optimized Delivery Time (hrs)	Optimized Customer Satisfaction (Rating 1-5)
1	140	Light	None	130	3.8	4
2	110	Light	Rain	120	3.2	4.5
3	160	Moderate	None	175	5.0	3.5
4	90	Light	None	100	2.0	5
5	180	Light	None	160	5.0	4

Explanation and Interpretation of Results:

- **Route ID 1**: The original route had a moderate traffic condition, resulting in a higher fuel cost and longer delivery time. After optimization, the route was shortened by 10 km, and the traffic condition improved to light, reducing both fuel cost and delivery time. Customer satisfaction improved due to faster delivery.

- **Route ID 2**: The optimization reduced the distance and adjusted for lighter traffic. Despite the rainy weather, fuel costs decreased, and delivery time was reduced. Customer satisfaction improved due to faster delivery times, even with the weather condition.

- **Route ID 3**: Originally, this route had heavy traffic and snowy conditions, leading to higher costs and longer delivery times. Optimization reduced the distance by 20 km and adjusted the weather to clear conditions, cutting fuel costs and reducing delivery time. However, customer satisfaction remained low compared to other routes due to the previous poor experience.

- **Route ID 4**: This route was already optimal with light traffic and no weather issues. The distance was slightly shortened, leading to a further reduction in fuel costs and delivery time. Customer satisfaction stayed at a high level.

- **Route ID 5**: Although this route was longer, optimization reduced its distance and improved traffic conditions, slightly lowering fuel costs and improving delivery time. Customer satisfaction increased slightly due to the improvement in overall performance.

Observations:

1. **Optimizing Traffic Conditions**: Routes with heavy traffic, like Route 3, experienced significant improvements after optimization, with reduced fuel costs and delivery times.

2. **Weather Consideration**: Routes that had weather challenges, like rain (Route 2) and snow (Route 3), benefitted from predictive models that adjusted for these factors, allowing better route planning.

3. **Distance and Time Reductions**: Most routes had their distances reduced, which directly led to lower fuel costs and faster delivery times. This improved operational efficiency.

4. **Customer Satisfaction**: Routes with faster delivery times and more predictable travel conditions saw improved customer satisfaction.

Supply Chain Management Decisions:

- **Route Optimization**: Invest in continuous data-driven optimization tools for route planning. Focus on reducing travel distances, avoiding traffic bottlenecks, and accounting for weather disruptions.

- **Fleet Management**: Adjust fleet assignment based on optimized routes to ensure resources are allocated to the most efficient routes, thus reducing costs.

- **Customer Experience Focus**: Given the positive correlation between faster delivery and customer satisfaction, prioritize optimization of the most critical routes where customers are most sensitive to delays.

- **Predictive Maintenance**: Integrate predictive maintenance systems to further reduce disruptions and ensure the fleet operates at peak efficiency on optimized routes.

By applying data science, the logistics company significantly improved fuel efficiency, reduced delivery times, and increased customer satisfaction, leading to enhanced profitability and better resource allocation.

2. Understanding Supply Chain Systems

A supply chain is the system of organizations, people, activities, information, and resources involved in moving a product or service from supplier to customer. It starts with the raw materials or components and moves through various stages like manufacturing, warehousing, and distribution, eventually reaching the consumer. The process is a network of suppliers, manufacturers, and distributors that work together to meet customer demand efficiently.

Effective supply chains aim to ensure that products are available when needed, at the right price, and in the right quantities. This requires careful planning and coordination. Companies rely on a mix of suppliers, logistics companies, and warehouses to make sure that goods flow smoothly. Inventory management, transportation, and communication are key factors in managing the flow of goods from the initial stages to the end consumer.

At the heart of a supply chain is the concept of demand and supply. The goal is to align production with customer demand, which can fluctuate. Companies use forecasting methods to predict demand patterns and plan their production accordingly. However, demand can change quickly, so supply chains need to be flexible and responsive to market shifts, which is why they invest in systems that monitor real-time data to adjust quickly when necessary.

One of the main challenges in supply chain management is balancing efficiency with resilience. A highly efficient supply chain aims to minimize costs and time, often through just-in-time inventory systems, which reduce the need to store large amounts of stock. However, this efficiency can come at the cost of vulnerability, as disruptions like natural disasters, geopolitical tensions, or pandemics can severely affect supply chains. Companies need to find ways to build in resilience to handle such disruptions.

Technological advancements have revolutionized supply chain management, enabling greater automation, real-time tracking, and data analysis. Tools like GPS, RFID, and blockchain help companies monitor goods as they move through the supply chain, providing transparency and allowing for quicker response times. These technologies also help optimize routes, reduce waste, and enhance coordination across different stages of the supply chain.

In today's global economy, supply chains have become increasingly complex and interconnected. Many companies source materials or products from different parts of the world, making coordination and communication more challenging. Global supply chains depend on multiple countries' infrastructure, trade regulations, and customs processes. This interconnectedness means that problems in one part of the world can quickly ripple across the entire chain, highlighting the importance of strategic planning, communication, and risk management in supply chain systems.

Practical Example: Understanding Supply Chain Systems from a Data Science Perspective

In a typical supply chain, data science can help optimize inventory levels, predict demand, and manage logistics. Let's consider a company that manufactures and sells electronic devices, and it wants to optimize its inventory based on historical sales data. The goal is to predict future demand and ensure that inventory levels match the forecast while minimizing both stockouts and overstock situations.

Sample Data (Sales and Inventory Data)

Month	Product A Sales	Product B Sales	Product A Inventory	Product B Inventory	Lead Time (Weeks)
January	500	300	1000	1200	2
February	550	320	950	1180	2
March	600	350	900	1150	3
April	650	380	850	1100	3
May	700	400	800	1050	4
June	750	450	750	1000	4

- Load the Data into a data analysis software / tool

- Analyze the data.

Example of a Data Science Approach

1. **Demand Forecasting**: By using time-series analysis (e.g., ARIMA, Exponential Smoothing), we can forecast future sales based on past sales trends. For simplicity, let's use a basic moving average (3-month) to forecast demand for the next month.

2. **Inventory Optimization**: Using a basic inventory model (e.g., Economic Order Quantity (EOQ) or Reorder Point formula), we can calculate when to reorder products and how much stock to hold.

Forecasting Output (3-Month Moving Average)

Month	Product A Sales	Product B Sales	Product A Forecast	Product B Forecast
January	500	300	-	-
February	550	320	-	-
March	600	350	550	323
April	650	380	600	350
May	700	400	616.67	366.67
June	750	450	650	400

Results and Interpretation

- **Forecast Accuracy**: The 3-month moving average method smooths out short-term fluctuations and provides a steady forecast for future demand. For instance, the forecasted sales for Product A in May are 616.67 units, which closely mirrors the actual sales trend.

- **Inventory Shortages**: Product A's inventory is steadily decreasing month over month, and without an adjustment in reordering, the company may face stockouts. The reorder point should be adjusted based on lead time and forecast demand.

- **Reordering Decisions**: For Product A, considering a 3-week lead time and forecast of 616.67 units for the next month, the reorder point should be calculated as:

$$Reorder\ Point = Forecasted\ Demand\ for\ Lead\ Time + Safety\ Stock$$

If safety stock is 10% of monthly demand (i.e., 62 units), then the reorder point would be:

Reorder Point=616.67×(34)+62≈496.25+62=558.25 units.

Thus, the company should reorder when inventory drops to approximately 558 units.

Observations

1. **Demand Trends**: Both Product A and Product B show increasing sales trends. This suggests the need to scale up production and adjust inventory levels to meet rising demand.

2. **Inventory Risk**: The decreasing inventory levels highlight the importance of timely reordering. If the company doesn't adjust its reorder quantities or timing, it risks stockouts, especially in June when sales are projected to increase further.

3. **Lead Time Impact**: Longer lead times (3-4 weeks) compound the need for earlier reordering, as seen with Product A.

Decisions from a Supply Chain Management Perspective

1. **Reorder Frequency**: Increase the frequency of inventory reviews, particularly for products with longer lead times (Product A and Product B), to prevent stockouts.

2. **Safety Stock Levels**: Adjust safety stock levels for higher-demand products (like Product A in May and June) to avoid disruptions.

3. **Production Scaling**: Scale up production based on forecasted demand. This can involve adjusting manufacturing schedules, increasing workforce, or procuring additional raw materials to meet forecasted needs.

4. **Data-Driven Adjustments**: Continuously refine forecasting models as more sales data becomes available to reduce forecasting errors and improve inventory management.

By leveraging data science techniques like demand forecasting, inventory management models, and continuous data analysis, the company can significantly improve its supply chain efficiency and responsiveness.

2.1 Basic Components of a Supply Chain

A supply chain is a network that involves the movement of goods, services, and information from the point of origin to the end customer. It starts with the procurement of raw materials, which are essential for creating products. Suppliers provide these raw materials, and their availability and quality play a significant role in ensuring that the manufacturing process runs smoothly. Companies must choose suppliers carefully, as they affect everything from cost to product quality and production timelines.

Once the materials are obtained, they are sent to manufacturers where the actual production takes place. Manufacturers use the raw materials to create finished products or components that will later be assembled or packaged. This process may involve multiple stages, including assembly, testing, and quality control, to ensure the final product meets the required specifications. Manufacturers often rely on technology and skilled workers to produce high-quality goods efficiently.

After production, the products need to be transported to distribution centers or warehouses. These facilities serve as storage locations where the products are held until they are needed by retailers or directly shipped to customers. The efficiency of warehousing operations, including the proper handling of goods, inventory management, and the ability to track products, plays a crucial role in reducing costs and improving delivery speeds.

Once the products are in the warehouse, they are distributed to retailers or other sales channels. Retailers play a critical role in the supply chain by making the products available to customers. They can sell directly to consumers or supply other businesses with goods. The coordination between manufacturers, wholesalers, and retailers is important to ensure that demand is met without overstocking or understocking products.

The last stage of the supply chain involves the end customer. Their demand drives the entire supply chain process, as companies work to meet customer expectations for product availability, quality, and delivery times. Customer feedback and buying patterns help companies forecast demand, manage inventory, and improve future production and distribution strategies. Meeting customer expectations is crucial for maintaining loyalty and ensuring repeat business.

Throughout all these stages, there are also several support functions, including logistics, information technology, and customer service. These functions ensure that products flow smoothly through the supply chain and that any issues are resolved quickly. Effective communication and coordination between all parties involved are necessary to keep the supply chain running efficiently and to prevent delays or disruptions that could negatively impact product availability or cost.

Practical Example: Breaking Down the Supply Chain of a Global Electronics Manufacturer

A global electronics manufacturer, such as a company that produces smartphones, operates across several continents, sourcing materials, components, and finished products from different regions. The company's supply chain involves raw material suppliers, component manufacturers, assembly plants, distribution centers, and retailers. Each step has specific lead times, costs, and risks associated with it. For this example, we'll break down the supply chain and assess the total cost and lead time to identify opportunities for optimization. We'll focus on key components like chips, displays, and batteries, sourced from different countries.

Sample Data:

Step	Supplier Location	Component	Lead Time (Days)	Cost per Unit (USD)	Quantity Ordered	Total Cost (USD)
Raw Material Procurement	China	Semiconductor Chip	15	10	1,000,000	10,000,000
Raw Material Procurement	South Korea	Display	10	8	1,000,000	8,000,000
Raw Material Procurement	Japan	Battery	12	5	1,000,000	5,000,000
Component Manufacturing	USA	Semiconductor Chip	8	12	1,000,000	12,000,000
Component Manufacturing	Vietnam	Display	7	7	1,000,000	7,000,000

Step	Supplier Location	Component	Lead Time (Days)	Cost per Unit (USD)	Quantity Ordered	Total Cost (USD)
Component Manufacturing	India	Battery	6	6	1,000,000	6,000,000
Assembly	Mexico	Final Assembly	14	20	1,000,000	20,000,000
Distribution	USA	Distribution	5	2	1,000,000	2,000,000

- Load the Data into a data analysis software / tool
- Analyze the data.

Output and Results:

The table above shows the supply chain breakdown with key data points for each step: lead time, cost per unit, quantity ordered, and total cost. By looking at the total cost per component and understanding the lead time, we can make several observations.

Explanation and Interpretation of Results:

1. **Lead Times and Costs**: The raw material procurement steps (chips from China, displays from South Korea, and batteries from Japan) have relatively long lead times (between 10–15 days). Manufacturing lead times are shorter, ranging from 6 to 8 days for battery manufacturing in India to 7–8 days for displays in Vietnam. Assembly in Mexico has the longest lead time of 14 days.

2. **Total Costs**: The cost per unit for chips is higher in the U.S. at $12 per unit compared to China at $10 per unit. Similarly, displays cost $8 in South Korea but only $7 in Vietnam. The batteries have a slight cost advantage when manufactured in India at $6 compared to $5 when sourced from Japan.

3. **Total Supply Chain Cost**: The total cost for producing and delivering 1,000,000 units is $70,000,000. The most expensive

stages are assembly in Mexico ($20 million) and chip procurement and manufacturing ($22 million combined).

Observations:

1. **Geographic Sourcing Costs**: Manufacturing the components in certain regions like the U.S. and South Korea is more expensive compared to alternatives like China, India, and Vietnam. This suggests an opportunity for cost reduction by shifting manufacturing or procurement locations.

2. **Lead Time Optimization**: While some regions have shorter lead times (e.g., India for batteries), others, like the U.S. and Mexico, contribute to longer total lead times. There may be an opportunity to streamline or consolidate suppliers to minimize delays and reduce risk.

3. **Cost vs. Lead Time Tradeoff**: There is a clear tradeoff between cost and lead time. For example, using U.S.-based suppliers for chips and displays provides quicker assembly times but comes at a higher cost, which could reduce profit margins.

Decisions from the Supply Chain Management Perspective:

1. **Outsource Component Manufacturing**: The company might consider shifting some manufacturing activities, such as semiconductor chip production, from the U.S. to China to lower costs. However, this could increase lead times, so tradeoffs must be considered.

2. **Supplier Consolidation**: The company could reduce complexity and improve lead time by consolidating suppliers. For example, sourcing chips and displays from the same region could reduce shipping time and costs.

3. **Nearshoring**: The company may look into nearshoring some of the assembly activities currently done in Mexico, possibly relocating it closer to markets like the U.S. to reduce shipping time and costs associated with long-distance logistics.

4. **Evaluate Transportation and Distribution Channels**: While distribution in the U.S. is cost-effective, the company may explore alternative distribution routes or optimize the flow of goods to reduce inventory costs.

By focusing on the tradeoff between lead time, cost, and inventory, the supply chain manager can make more informed decisions that balance cost savings with service levels and customer satisfaction.

2.2 Types of Supply Chain Models

Supply chain models refer to the various strategies that companies adopt to manage the flow of goods, services, and information from suppliers to consumers. One common model is the make-to-stock (MTS) approach, where products are manufactured in advance based on predicted demand. Companies following this model typically produce large quantities of goods and store them in warehouses until customers place orders. This model works well for products with stable demand and allows businesses to quickly respond to orders, but it carries the risk of overproduction or stockouts if demand is misjudged.

Another widely used model is the make-to-order (MTO) approach, which is the opposite of MTS. In this case, products are only manufactured after receiving a customer's order. This helps to reduce inventory costs, as no goods are produced until there is a confirmed demand. However, it can result in longer lead times, since customers must wait for the product to be produced before it can be shipped. Companies that deal with customized or highly variable products often adopt this model to avoid the costs and risks associated with large inventories.

The assemble-to-order (ATO) model sits between make-to-stock and make-to-order. It involves producing subassemblies or components in advance, but final products are only put together once an order is placed. This allows for some level of customization while maintaining shorter lead times than make-to-order systems. It is commonly used in industries like computers and electronics, where the base parts are standardized but final configurations differ depending on customer preferences. The key challenge in this model is ensuring the availability of various components to assemble the final product quickly.

In contrast, the engineer-to-order (ETO) model is used for highly specialized products that require significant customization based on specific customer needs. Products are designed and engineered from scratch once an order is received. This model is typical in industries like construction, aerospace, and heavy machinery, where each product is unique and requires extensive engineering input. Lead times are often very long, and the complexity of managing engineering, procurement, and manufacturing processes can be a significant challenge.

The vendor-managed inventory (VMI) model shifts the responsibility for managing inventory to the supplier. In this model, the supplier monitors the inventory levels at the customer's location and takes the necessary actions to replenish stock. This approach can lead to cost savings for both parties, as it reduces the risk of stockouts and minimizes inventory management overhead for the customer. However, it requires a high level of trust and collaboration between the supplier and the customer to ensure accurate data sharing and timely replenishment.

The continuous replenishment model (CRP) is a variant of the VMI model that emphasizes automatic and regular restocking of products based on predefined schedules or real-time sales data. This model is especially effective in industries where demand is predictable, such as groceries or fast-moving consumer goods. By continuously replenishing stock, businesses can reduce the chance of stockouts and ensure that products are always available when customers need them. However, it can also lead to inefficiencies if demand fluctuates unexpectedly or if the replenishment system is not properly managed.

Practical Example: Choosing Between Push and Pull Models in a Food Distribution System

In a food distribution system, a company needs to decide between using a **Push** or **Pull** model for managing inventory and delivering products to retailers. A Push model involves forecasting demand and producing inventory in advance, whereas a Pull model relies on actual demand at the point of sale (e.g., grocery stores) to trigger replenishment orders. The company has a warehouse that supplies three types of perishable food items (e.g., apples, bread, and milk) to five stores, and the decision will influence stock levels, replenishment speed, and overall inventory costs.

Sample Data:

Item	Average Daily Demand (Units)	Lead Time (Days)	Warehouse Stock (Units)	Retailer 1 Demand (Units)	Retailer 2 Demand (Units)	Retailer 3 Demand (Units)	Retailer 4 Demand (Units)	Retailer 5 Demand (Units)
Apples	100	2	500	80	120	90	100	110
Bread	150	1	300	130	140	160	120	150
Milk	200	3	600	180	190	210	200	210

Push Model Output:

Under the **Push** model, the company will forecast demand and maintain a buffer stock at the warehouse based on estimated sales. Since the company knows the average daily demand, it will preemptively ship quantities to stores based on these forecasts. If lead time is 2-3 days, restocking will occur even if actual demand does not align perfectly with forecasts.

Item	Forecasted Demand (Units)	Stock Shipped to Retailers	Total Inventory at Warehouse	Potential Surplus/Shortfall
Apples	100/day	500 (to cover 5 stores)	500	No surplus, potential shortfall for Store 2
Bread	150/day	750 (to cover 5 stores)	300	Surplus in the warehouse
Milk	200/day	1000 (to cover 5 stores)	600	Surplus in the warehouse

Pull Model Output:

In the **Pull** model, replenishment happens based on actual sales data. If one store experiences higher demand, the warehouse will prioritize that store's needs, reducing the risk of overstocking and understocking at any particular store.

Item	Actual Sales (Units)	Stock Replenished to Retailers	Total Inventory at Warehouse	Surplus/Shortfall Observations
Apples	480	480	500	Close to forecasted demand, minimal surplus
Bread	780	780	300	Overstock risk at the warehouse
Milk	950	950	600	Slight shortfall for Stores 2 and 5

Explanation and Interpretation:

- **Push Model Results**: The warehouse is stocked with excess inventory for certain items (especially bread and milk), leading to overstocking in the warehouse, which can incur additional storage costs. However, this method reduces the risk of stockouts at the stores. The main issue is the potential shortfall in apples at Store 2 due to fluctuations in demand. This could lead to lost sales or customer dissatisfaction.

- **Pull Model Results**: The pull model adjusts to actual sales, reducing the risk of overstocking. In this case, the milk item faced a slight shortfall, which could have led to missed sales, but overall, there's a more efficient allocation of inventory to meet store-specific demand. However, there's a risk of understocking in situations of lead time delays or unpredicted demand spikes.

Observations:

1. **Push Model**: There is a tendency toward overstocking or understocking since forecasts do not always match actual demand. It can lead to inefficiencies in inventory storage and higher operational costs.

2. **Pull Model**: Although there is more alignment with actual demand, there is a risk of shortfalls and missed sales due to the lead time required for replenishment. It requires a highly responsive system and close monitoring of sales data.

Supply Chain Management Decision:

- **Push Model**: Suitable when demand is relatively predictable, or for products with longer shelf life. It helps ensure availability across all locations, but requires careful balancing of stock levels to avoid excess inventory costs.

- **Pull Model**: More appropriate when demand is highly variable or for perishable items (like milk and bread). The pull model can be more cost-effective by reducing excess inventory and minimizing storage costs, but requires a more agile system with quick response times.

In this case, the **Pull Model** would likely be the better choice for the perishable food items, as it minimizes wastage and ensures that inventory levels match actual sales demand, especially when the company has robust demand forecasting and rapid replenishment capabilities.

2.3 The Role of Data in Supply Chain Optimization

Data plays a crucial role in supply chain optimization by providing the visibility and insights needed to make informed decisions. Supply chains are often complex, involving multiple stakeholders, processes, and logistics, and data helps to streamline these elements by offering accurate and up-to-date information. Through continuous data collection, companies can monitor their entire supply chain operations, from procurement and inventory management to distribution and customer service, ensuring they remain efficient and responsive to changes in demand or external disruptions.

By leveraging data, businesses can improve demand forecasting, which is a critical component of supply chain planning. Historical sales data, market trends, and consumer behavior can be analyzed to predict future demand more accurately. This helps prevent stockouts or overstock situations, reducing unnecessary inventory costs and ensuring that customers receive products when they need them. Better forecasting leads to optimized production schedules, fewer delays, and a more balanced supply chain.

Data also enhances the ability to track and manage inventory in real time. With the help of technologies like RFID, barcode scanning, and IoT sensors, companies can monitor inventory levels at different stages of the supply chain. This constant flow of information allows businesses to make adjustments on the fly, reorder products in time, and even automate certain inventory management tasks. This level of control improves efficiency and reduces the risks of holding excessive stock or running into shortages.

In addition, data supports supplier relationship management by providing performance metrics that help businesses identify reliable partners. By analyzing delivery times, quality levels, and other supplier-related data, companies can make more strategic decisions about which suppliers to prioritize or switch from. This data-driven approach fosters stronger collaboration and can help companies negotiate better terms, ultimately leading to a more resilient supply chain.

Transportation management is another area where data significantly impacts optimization. By analyzing transportation routes, fuel costs, vehicle performance, and delivery schedules, companies can improve the efficiency of their logistics operations. Data allows businesses to optimize delivery routes, consolidate shipments, and reduce transportation costs, all while ensuring timely deliveries to customers. This level of optimization can significantly lower the overall operational costs of the supply chain.

Finally, data enhances decision-making and risk management across the supply chain. In times of disruption, such as natural disasters or geopolitical events, companies can use real-time data to assess the impact and quickly adjust their strategies. For example, if a particular route or supplier becomes unavailable, data can help companies identify alternative sources or distribution routes. By integrating data into their risk management frameworks, businesses can ensure that they are prepared for unforeseen events, improving the resilience and flexibility of their supply chains.

Practical Example: Leveraging Historical Sales Data to Optimize Supplier Orders for a Fashion Retailer

A fashion retailer wants to optimize its supplier orders using historical sales data. The retailer has historical sales data over the past six months for a specific line of summer dresses and wants to forecast future demand and improve order accuracy. By analyzing this historical data, the retailer can estimate the amount of inventory to order from suppliers, ensuring they meet customer demand while minimizing excess stock. The table below shows sales data for the summer dresses, including the number of units sold per week and the order quantity made at the start of each month. The retailer is now trying to improve their ordering process based on this data.

Sample Data:

Week	Units Sold	Supplier Order Quantity	Week 1	Week 2	Week 3	Week 4	Week 5	Week 6
1	50	60	50	55	58	60	45	65
2	60	70	60	65	67	70	55	68
3	65	75	65	60	63	70	68	75
4	70	80	70	75	72	80	72	80
5	55	65	55	53	60	65	50	60
6	60	70	60	62	65	68	63	65

- Load the Data into a data analysis software / tool

- Analyze the data.

Output:

After analyzing the historical sales data, the following adjustments can be made to optimize the order quantities:

- **Demand Forecasting**: Using moving averages of past sales (e.g., 3-week average), the retailer forecasts an average weekly demand of 60 units.

- **Supplier Order Optimization**: Based on the forecast, the retailer adjusts future order quantities to avoid over-ordering while meeting demand.

Adjusted Order Quantities:

Week	Units Sold	Original Order Quantity	Adjusted Order Quantity
1	50	60	55
2	60	70	65
3	65	75	70
4	70	80	75
5	55	65	60
6	60	70	65

Interpretation and Analysis:

1. **Demand Forecasting**: The forecasted demand is 60 units per week, which aligns closely with the average sales over the past six weeks. This insight suggests that maintaining a weekly order of 60 units would suffice for future sales.

2. **Order Quantity Adjustment**: The retailer has adjusted the order quantities based on the sales trend. For instance, in Week 1, where actual sales were lower than expected, the order was reduced from 60 to 55 units. This prevents excess stock from accumulating and reduces holding costs.

3. **Optimization Strategy**: The adjusted order quantities for Weeks 2 to 4 reflect a slight decrease from the original order. This aligns with the goal of minimizing overstock without risking stockouts, based on the forecasted demand of 60 units.

Observations:

- Weeks with sales higher than the forecast (e.g., Week 4) show an adjusted order quantity of 75, which ensures demand is met without significant delay or stockouts.

- Weeks with lower sales than forecast (e.g., Week 1 and Week 5) show a reduction in order quantity, helping the retailer avoid overstock and related storage costs.

Supply Chain Management Decisions:

- **Forecast Accuracy**: It's essential to regularly update forecasts based on sales trends. The retailer may want to implement a more sophisticated model, like exponential smoothing or machine learning, for improved demand prediction.

- **Supplier Relationships**: Collaborating with suppliers to adjust order quantities in real time based on sales data can help reduce lead times and costs. This would help ensure that orders are placed just in time to avoid stockouts or excess inventory.

- **Inventory Levels**: The retailer should monitor stock levels closely and adjust orders as needed, factoring in seasonality, promotions, and upcoming trends. Reducing stockouts is crucial for customer satisfaction, while minimizing excess stock reduces financial strain from overstocked inventory.

3. Data Collection and Management

Data collection and management are essential processes in any research or business operation. Data collection refers to the process of gathering information from various sources to support analysis, decision-making, or reporting. It can be done through surveys, interviews, observations, or by extracting data from existing records or databases. The quality of the data collected is crucial for ensuring that the conclusions drawn from it are valid and reliable. Careful planning and the use of appropriate methods for data collection can significantly impact the success of a project or study.

Once the data is collected, it needs to be organized and stored effectively for easy access and analysis. Data management involves organizing, storing, and maintaining data in a way that allows it to be retrieved and used efficiently. This includes determining the appropriate format, structure, and storage systems for the data. Proper data management helps reduce errors, duplication, and data loss. It ensures that the information is readily available for use when needed, and that it remains consistent and up-to-date.

Effective data management also involves setting up protocols for data security and privacy. This is especially important when handling sensitive or personal data. Secure data storage, regular backups, and controlled access are essential to protect against unauthorized access or data breaches. Compliance with privacy regulations and data protection laws is a fundamental part of managing data, particularly in sectors like healthcare, finance, and education. This aspect of data management ensures that both the integrity and confidentiality of the data are preserved.

In addition to security, data quality is another critical aspect of data management. Data should be accurate, consistent, and free from errors. Establishing standards for data entry and validation procedures can help ensure the integrity of the information. Regular audits and data cleansing processes are important for identifying and correcting discrepancies or outdated information. By maintaining high data quality, organizations can make better decisions based on reliable and trustworthy information.

Data collection and management processes must also adapt to changing technological environments. With the increasing use of digital tools, automation, and artificial intelligence, data management practices have become more complex. New systems and software solutions are being developed to handle large volumes of data, perform real-time analysis, and integrate data from multiple sources. Organizations must keep pace with these advancements to remain efficient and competitive. Adapting to new technologies can lead to improvements in data accuracy, accessibility, and speed.

Finally, the proper use of data collection and management strategies can significantly improve business operations or research outcomes. By ensuring that data is collected systematically, organized efficiently, and protected properly, organizations can derive valuable insights that drive innovation and informed decision-making. Clear data management policies also facilitate collaboration between departments, stakeholders, or researchers. Ultimately, effective data collection and management provide the foundation for success in any data-driven initiative.

Practical Example: Data Collection and Management in Supply Chain Management

Context: A company is tracking the delivery times for its suppliers to understand their performance and optimize the supply chain. The company collects data on the order date, delivery date, and product type from five suppliers over a month. The objective is to identify which suppliers are consistently meeting delivery deadlines and which might need improvement.

Sample Data Table:

Supplier	Order Date	Delivery Date	Product Type	Days Late (Delivery - Order)
Supplier A	01/01/2025	03/01/2025	Electronics	2
Supplier B	01/01/2025	04/01/2025	Furniture	3
Supplier C	02/01/2025	04/01/2025	Electronics	2
Supplier D	02/01/2025	03/01/2025	Furniture	1
Supplier E	03/01/2025	06/01/2025	Electronics	3

Output:

- Average days late: 2.2
- Supplier performance analysis:

- Supplier A: 2 days late
- Supplier B: 3 days late
- Supplier C: 2 days late
- Supplier D: 1 day late
- Supplier E: 3 days late

Interpretation of Results:

- **Supplier D** is the most punctual, with only 1 day of delay on average.
- **Suppliers B and E** are the least reliable, with 3 days of delay each.
- The average delay across all suppliers is 2.2 days, which is a concern for the company if the goal is to have timely deliveries to meet production schedules.

Discussion of Observations:

- Supplier D stands out as a reliable supplier, so it might be worth increasing their orders or building a stronger relationship with them.
- Suppliers B and E have more significant delays, suggesting the company should evaluate their processes, such as production or logistics inefficiencies, and consider renegotiating delivery terms or even switching suppliers for certain products.
- Overall, if timely deliveries are crucial for the company's operations, they may need to reconsider supplier relationships or improve inventory buffers.

Decisions from a Supply Chain Management Perspective:

- **Supplier Performance Monitoring**: Implement a more robust supplier performance monitoring system with regular check-ins.
- **Supplier Management**: Focus on improving communication and delivery schedules with Suppliers B and E. Consider diversifying the supply base for critical products.
- **Contingency Planning**: Develop contingency plans for delays, such as maintaining a safety stock or negotiating penalty clauses in contracts.
- **Long-Term Strategy**: Suppliers with consistent delays (B and E) could be put on probation or phased out if no improvements are observed. Alternatively, finding new suppliers who can meet delivery deadlines could be prioritized.

3.1 Sources of Supply Chain Data

Supply chain data can be gathered from a variety of sources, each playing a critical role in ensuring efficient operations. One of the most common sources is transaction data, which includes information related to sales, purchases, inventory levels, and shipments. This data typically comes from enterprise resource planning (ERP) systems or point-of-sale (POS) systems, providing real-time insights into stock movements, demand, and sales trends. Transactional data helps businesses track performance and manage resources effectively, providing the foundation for more informed decision-making.

Supplier data is another crucial source of supply chain information. It includes details about suppliers' capabilities, delivery performance, pricing, and lead times. This data often comes from vendor management systems or supplier portals, where businesses track their relationships with suppliers. Having access to accurate supplier data allows companies to evaluate supplier reliability, identify potential risks, and optimize procurement processes to reduce costs and avoid delays.

Logistics and transportation data also contribute significantly to supply chain management. This data comes from transportation management systems (TMS), GPS tracking, and third-party logistics (3PL) providers. It encompasses information on delivery times, route efficiency, fuel consumption, and carrier performance. Companies use this data to monitor and optimize transportation routes, reduce costs, and improve delivery reliability, ensuring that products reach their destinations on time and in good condition.

Inventory data is another vital source of supply chain information. This includes real-time stock levels, stock movements, and inventory turnover rates. Warehouse management systems (WMS) and barcode scanning technology help collect this data, providing visibility into stock levels across various locations. Accurate inventory data ensures that companies can maintain optimal stock levels, reduce excess inventory, and avoid stockouts, leading to better demand forecasting and improved customer satisfaction.

Customer data is also essential for understanding demand and improving service levels. This data is collected from customer relationship management (CRM) systems, e-commerce platforms, and feedback surveys. It includes information on customer preferences, purchasing behavior, and order histories. By analyzing customer data, businesses can better forecast demand, personalize offerings, and enhance their marketing and sales strategies, ensuring that products are available when and where customers need them.

Finally, external data sources such as market trends, economic indicators, and weather data play an important role in supply chain decision-making. This type of data can be collected from government reports, industry publications, market research firms, or specialized data providers. By incorporating external data, companies can anticipate changes in demand, plan for disruptions, and make proactive adjustments to their supply chains, ensuring that they remain competitive and resilient in the face of unforeseen challenges.

This is a comprehensive breakdown of the critical data sources in supply chain management. Each type of data serves a unique purpose and is essential for different aspects of optimization:

- **Transaction Data**: Central for real-time monitoring and decision-making, it provides insights into sales, inventory, and demand fluctuations. It's foundational for understanding operational performance.

- **Supplier Data**: Important for vendor management, allowing businesses to evaluate supplier performance and reliability, which is crucial for risk management and cost optimization.

- **Logistics and Transportation Data**: Essential for optimizing transportation costs, delivery times, and route planning. It enables companies to maintain service levels and reduce inefficiencies in the delivery process.

- **Inventory Data**: Helps businesses track stock movements and manage their warehouse efficiently, ensuring that inventory levels align with demand, which prevents overstocking or stockouts.

- **Customer Data**: Critical for demand forecasting and personalizing products and services to customers. By analyzing customer data, businesses can enhance marketing and product offerings, directly influencing sales.

- **External Data**: Provides the broader context within which supply chains operate. External factors such as market trends, weather patterns, and economic shifts can significantly impact supply chain decisions and are essential for proactive planning.

By integrating these data sources effectively, businesses can enhance their supply chain resilience, reduce costs, and improve customer satisfaction, ultimately driving operational excellence and competitive advantage.

3.2 Data Quality and Integrity Issues

Data quality and integrity are fundamental to effective decision-making, as poor-quality data can lead to inaccurate conclusions and flawed strategies. When data is incomplete, outdated, or inconsistent, it reduces its value and reliability. Ensuring that data is accurate, consistent, and complete is crucial to avoid errors that could affect operational processes or lead to misinformed decisions. Any discrepancies in data, whether caused by human error, system malfunction, or poor data entry practices, undermine the credibility of the information being used.

One of the primary challenges in maintaining data integrity is ensuring the consistency of data across different systems. When multiple departments or organizations use different methods of data collection and storage, there is a risk that the same information may be recorded in various ways, causing confusion and inconsistency. This can lead to discrepancies between databases, resulting in incomplete or inaccurate reports that may affect business operations or compliance with regulations.

Another common issue is the lack of proper data validation processes. Without robust mechanisms in place to verify the accuracy and quality of data during input, erroneous data can easily make its way into systems. This often occurs when data is entered manually, leaving room for human mistakes. In some cases, the data may be outdated, reflecting past conditions that no longer apply, which can distort analysis and forecasts. It is essential to implement automated checks or validation rules to ensure that data meets predefined quality standards before it enters a system.

In addition to errors that occur during data entry, data corruption and loss are significant threats to data integrity. This can happen due to hardware failure, software glitches, or cyberattacks. When data is corrupted or lost, organizations may struggle to recover or rebuild essential information, leading to significant downtime or loss of productivity. Ensuring that proper backup protocols are in place is crucial to mitigate the risks associated with data loss and corruption.

Data privacy and security issues also affect data quality and integrity. Sensitive information, such as personal or financial data, must be protected from unauthorized access or tampering. If this data is compromised, it can lead to not only a loss of trust but also legal and financial consequences. To maintain both data security and integrity, organizations must implement strong encryption methods, access controls, and monitoring systems to safeguard their data from potential threats.

Finally, organizations must continually monitor and audit their data quality and integrity practices to identify potential issues and address them proactively. Regular assessments help ensure that data remains accurate, consistent, and up to date. Failure to address data quality and integrity concerns can have long-term negative impacts on an organization, undermining its operations, damaging its reputation, and hindering its ability to make informed decisions. By prioritizing data quality and integrity, organizations can build a solid foundation for success and mitigate the risks associated with poor data management.

Practical Example: Addressing Missing Data and Outliers in Supplier Lead Time Records

In supply chain management, it's crucial to have accurate supplier lead time records to ensure timely delivery and effective inventory management. However, missing data and outliers in the lead time records can distort decision-making and forecasting accuracy. For example, consider a dataset of lead times (in days) for a supplier over the past 12 months. There are a few missing entries, and some lead times appear to be unusually long (outliers) due to shipping delays.

Sample Data (Before Cleaning)

Month	Lead Time (Days)
January	12
February	10
March	15
April	NULL
May	200
June	8
July	9
August	NULL
September	10
October	50

Month	Lead Time (Days)
November	12
December	14

- Load the Data into a data analysis software / tool

- Analyze the data.

Steps for Handling Missing Data and Outliers:

1. **Addressing Missing Data:**
   - We use **mean imputation** to replace missing values. The mean lead time is calculated from the available data points: Mean = (12 + 10 + 15 + 8 + 9 + 10 + 50 + 12 + 14) / 9 = 12.22 days (rounded to 2 decimal places).
   - The missing values for April and August are replaced with 12.22 days.

2. **Addressing Outliers:**
   - Outliers are typically defined as values that are more than 1.5 times the interquartile range (IQR) above the third quartile or below the first quartile. For simplicity, we decide that any lead time greater than 30 days is an outlier and should be adjusted.
   - The outliers in May (200 days) and October (50 days) are replaced by the median of the dataset (which is 12 days).

Cleaned Data (After Handling Missing Data and Outliers)

Month	Lead Time (Days)
January	12
February	10
March	15
April	12.22
May	12

Month	Lead Time (Days)
June	8
July	9
August	12.22
September	10
October	12
November	12
December	14

Explanation and Interpretation of Results:

- **Missing Data**: The missing values in April and August were imputed with the mean lead time of 12.22 days. This approach assumes the missing data is missing at random and uses available information to fill gaps. Though not perfect, this provides a reasonable estimate without distorting the overall trend too much.

- **Outliers**: The outliers in May (200 days) and October (50 days) were replaced by the median lead time of 12 days. This action removes extreme values that could significantly skew the analysis or lead to incorrect decision-making, such as inaccurate supplier performance evaluation or over-ordering stock to buffer against supposed long delays.

Observations:

- After addressing the missing data and outliers, the cleaned dataset now provides a more consistent representation of lead times.

- Lead times now range between 8 and 15 days, with a central tendency around 12 days, which suggests that the supplier's typical performance is fairly stable, barring some minor variation.

Supply Chain Management Decisions:

1. **Forecasting and Planning**: With the cleaned data, supply chain planners can confidently forecast supplier lead times, as the data now reflects realistic delivery times.

2. **Supplier Performance Evaluation**: The removal of outliers helps to better evaluate the supplier's performance, ensuring that extreme values due to one-off issues don't distort overall performance metrics.

3. **Inventory Management**: Accurate lead time information enables better inventory management decisions, such as determining reorder points and safety stock levels to avoid stockouts without overstocking.

4. **Supplier Relationship**: If the supplier consistently exhibits long lead times or extreme variability, further investigation into their supply chain processes may be warranted. Identifying trends or causes of delays could lead to discussions for improvement or alternative sourcing.

By effectively managing missing data and outliers, the supply chain team ensures that their decisions are based on accurate and reliable data, ultimately leading to improved supplier management and operational efficiency.

3.3 Data Warehousing and Management Techniques

Data warehousing is the process of collecting, storing, and managing large amounts of data from various sources to enable efficient querying and analysis. It involves consolidating data from different systems into a central repository, often referred to as a data warehouse. This centralized storage allows businesses to access data from multiple areas, such as sales, marketing, and finance, in one place, making it easier to analyze trends and make informed decisions. The data stored in a warehouse is typically structured and optimized for querying and reporting, rather than operational tasks.

Data management techniques within a warehouse focus on organizing and maintaining the integrity of data over time. This process includes data cleaning, where inconsistencies and errors are identified and corrected, ensuring that the information is reliable and accurate. Additionally, data is often transformed during the extraction process to fit the warehouse's schema, making it more uniform and easier to work with. These techniques help ensure that users have access to high-quality, consistent data for their analysis needs.

A critical aspect of data warehousing is the concept of ETL, which stands for Extract, Transform, and Load. ETL processes are used to move data from the source systems into the data warehouse. During extraction, data is pulled from its original source. Transformation refers to the processes of cleaning, formatting, and structuring the data so that it is usable. Finally, loading involves placing the transformed data into the warehouse. These processes are essential to ensure that data is up-to-date and ready for analysis.

Another important aspect of data management in a warehouse is maintaining data security and privacy. Since the data warehouse stores sensitive and valuable information, organizations implement access controls and encryption to protect the data from unauthorized use or breaches. Managing user roles and permissions ensures that only authorized individuals have access to the specific data they need for analysis, helping to minimize security risks. Additionally, organizations must adhere to legal and regulatory requirements concerning data privacy, ensuring compliance with laws like GDPR or HIPAA.

Data warehousing techniques also emphasize the importance of data scalability and performance. As the volume of data grows, it becomes necessary to design the warehouse in a way that can scale to handle large datasets without compromising performance. Data is often partitioned, indexed, or archived to maintain query performance. Additionally, technologies like cloud storage are increasingly used to store and process large volumes of data, offering flexibility and reducing the burden on on-premise infrastructure.

In addition to storing and managing data, data warehouses support advanced analytics, business intelligence, and reporting. They are designed to enable users to run complex queries and generate insights that drive business decisions. By integrating data from various sources, companies can gain a comprehensive view of their operations, allowing them to identify patterns, forecast trends, and make data-driven strategic decisions. As business needs evolve, so too must the data warehousing techniques, ensuring that the system remains adaptable and capable of supporting new data sources and analysis tools.

Practical Example: Designing a Data Warehouse to Integrate Sales, Inventory, and Supplier Data

A company sells various electronic products across different regions. The company maintains separate systems for sales transactions, inventory levels, and supplier information. The goal is to design a data warehouse to integrate data from these disparate systems to improve decision-making and optimize supply chain operations. The company aims to analyze sales trends, inventory turnover, and supplier performance to ensure stock levels align with demand, identify slow-moving products, and streamline procurement strategies.

Sample Data

Product ID	Product Name	Region	Sales Quantity	Sales Revenue	Inventory Level	Supplier ID	Supplier Name	Lead Time (days)	Supplier Cost	Reorder Level
101	Laptop	East	500	250,000	100	1	Supplier A	7	500	50
102	Smartphone	West	700	210,000	150	2	Supplier B	14	300	100

Product ID	Product Name	Region	Sales Quantity	Sales Revenue	Inventory Level	Supplier ID	Supplier Name	Lead Time (days)	Supplier Cost	Reorder Level
103	Headphones	North	300	30,000	80	3	Supplier C	10	50	30
104	Tablet	South	200	40,000	120	4	Supplier D	5	200	20
105	Smartwatch	East	150	22,500	50	1	Supplier A	7	150	40

- Load the Data into a data analysis software / tool
- Analyze the data.

Data Warehouse Design Approach

1. **Fact Table**: Store data related to sales transactions, inventory levels, and product movements.

   o Fact tables would include fields like Product ID, Sales Quantity, Sales Revenue, and Inventory Level.

2. **Dimension Tables**:

   o **Product Dimension**: Contains product details like Product ID, Product Name.

   o **Time Dimension**: Stores time-related data (dates, months, quarters, years).

   o **Region Dimension**: Captures sales region information.

   o **Supplier Dimension**: Includes data on supplier names, costs, and lead times.

Output and Results

Using the integrated data warehouse, we can analyze sales, inventory, and supply chain performance.

Prod uct ID	Product Name	Regi on	Sales Quan tity	Sales Reve nue	Invent ory Level	Suppl ier Name	Suppl ier Cost	Lea d Tim e (da ys)	Reor der Level	Sales to Invent ory Ratio	Stock out Risk (Days)
101	Laptop	East	500	250,0 00	100	Suppl ier A	500	7	50	5.0	7
102	Smartph one	West	700	210,0 00	150	Suppl ier B	300	14	100	4.67	14
103	Headph ones	Nort h	300	30,00 0	80	Suppl ier C	50	10	30	3.75	10
104	Tablet	Sout h	200	40,00 0	120	Suppl ier D	200	5	20	1.67	20
105	Smartw atch	East	150	22,50 0	50	Suppl ier A	150	7	40	3.0	7

Explanation and Interpretation of Results

1. **Sales to Inventory Ratio**: This ratio measures the efficiency of inventory turnover. A higher ratio indicates better sales efficiency relative to inventory levels. For example:

   o The **Laptop** has a sales-to-inventory ratio of 5.0, meaning it's selling quickly and inventory is relatively low.

   o The **Tablet**, with a ratio of 1.67, is moving slower than the Laptop and might indicate excess stock or reduced demand.

2. **Stockout Risk (Days)**: This measure estimates how many days of sales can be fulfilled with the current inventory before running out of stock. A lower stockout risk suggests better inventory planning.

   o **Smartphone** and **Laptop** have a stockout risk of 7 and 7 days, respectively, meaning inventory may run out within a week, indicating the need for restocking soon.

   o **Tablet**, with a stockout risk of 20 days, has a lower immediate risk of stockouts, but may indicate slower-moving inventory that needs attention in terms of sales or promotions.

Observations and Decisions from a Supply Chain Management Perspective

1. **Inventory Optimization**:

   o The **Laptop** and **Smartwatch** have relatively low inventory levels, but their sales-to-inventory ratios suggest high demand. These products may need to be restocked frequently to avoid stockouts.

   o **Tablet** has slower sales, and its higher stockout risk could be mitigated by reducing inventory levels or finding ways to boost demand (e.g., promotions or discounts).

2. **Supplier Management**:

   o The **Smartphone** and **Headphones** rely on suppliers with longer lead times (14 and 10 days, respectively). Supply chain managers should plan ahead for these products, particularly considering their sales volumes and inventory levels. Longer lead times increase the risk of stockouts if demand spikes unexpectedly.

   o **Supplier A** is used for both **Laptop** and **Smartwatch**, and both products have lower lead times (7 days), providing quicker replenishment. However, the company should monitor the supplier's capacity to ensure timely deliveries.

3. **Reordering and Procurement Strategy**:

   o Based on the **Reorder Levels**, products like **Smartphone** and **Laptop** should be prioritized for reorder. The company should consider increasing order quantities for high-demand products to ensure timely restocking and minimize the risk of stockouts.

   o For slower-moving products like the **Tablet**, the company may consider reducing reorder levels or negotiating with the supplier for better pricing, given the higher costs relative to sales.

By integrating these insights, the company can improve its inventory management, supplier relationships, and demand forecasting, ultimately leading to more efficient supply chain operations and better customer satisfaction.

4. Data Preprocessing for Supply Chain Analytics

Data preprocessing is an essential step in supply chain analytics, as it ensures the data is clean, consistent, and usable for analysis. The first step typically involves gathering data from various sources, including suppliers, manufacturers, distributors, and customers. These sources often include different formats and structures, such as spreadsheets, databases, or transactional logs, making it necessary to standardize the data. By aligning all data to a common format, organizations can effectively integrate and analyze the information across the entire supply chain.

Once the data is collected, the next critical task is cleaning it to remove inconsistencies, inaccuracies, and missing values. Incomplete or incorrect data can lead to misleading insights and poor decision-making. Data cleaning involves identifying missing values, correcting errors, and dealing with duplicates. In supply chain analytics, this may include tasks like filling in missing order quantities or correcting product codes that have been entered incorrectly. Ensuring data quality is crucial for producing reliable analysis and actionable results.

Data transformation is another important stage, where raw data is converted into a more useful and structured format. In supply chain contexts, this could involve converting timestamps to a uniform time zone, aggregating data into relevant categories (like weekly or monthly sales), or normalizing data to ensure consistency in units of measurement. Data transformation ensures that the data is aligned with the specific needs of the analysis, allowing for better insights into inventory levels, order fulfillment, and supplier performance.

Another vital aspect of preprocessing is feature engineering, where new variables are created from the existing data to improve predictive models. In the supply chain, this might involve calculating the lead time between orders and shipments or deriving seasonal trends from sales data. By generating new features that provide more context or highlight underlying patterns, organizations can better understand complex supply chain dynamics and improve their forecasting and optimization efforts.

Data integration is also a key component of preprocessing. Supply chain data often comes from multiple systems—such as Enterprise Resource Planning (ERP) systems, Customer Relationship Management (CRM) platforms, and external data sources like weather or market trends. Integrating these diverse datasets into a unified system allows analysts to gain a holistic view of the supply chain. This integration helps uncover relationships between variables that might not be apparent when looking at individual data sources.

Finally, data scaling and normalization can be necessary, especially when preparing data for machine learning models or optimization algorithms. Supply chain data can vary widely in magnitude, such as order quantities compared to shipping distances or production costs. Scaling ensures that no single feature dominates the analysis, allowing models to treat each variable on equal footing. This helps improve the accuracy and effectiveness of the model, ensuring that predictions and decisions are based on all relevant aspects of the supply chain.

Practical Example:

In this example, we consider a retail company managing a supply chain for various products across multiple stores. The company needs to preprocess its data before performing any advanced analytics, such as demand forecasting and inventory optimization. The dataset contains information about sales, stock levels, and delivery times across different regions, but there are issues with missing data, outliers, and inconsistent formats. The goal of preprocessing is to clean the data so that it can be used for effective decision-making in the supply chain process.

Sample Data:

Store_ID	Product_ID	Sales_Qty	Stock_Level	Delivery_Time (days)	Date	Region
S001	P001	120	50	5	2024-01-01	North
S002	P002	80	30	7	2024-01-02	South
S001	P003	NULL	40	4	2024-01-03	North
S003	P001	150	60	NULL	2024-01-04	East
S002	P002	90	25	6	2024-01-05	South

Store_ID	Product_ID	Sales_Qty	Stock_Level	Delivery_Time (days)	Date	Region
S001	P001	110	NULL	5	2024-01-06	North
S003	P003	130	45	3	2024-01-07	East

- Load the Data into a data analysis software / tool
- Analyze the data.

Steps of Data Preprocessing:

1. **Handle Missing Data:**
   - Fill missing Sales_Qty using the median sales for the corresponding product and store.
   - Fill missing Stock_Level using the average stock for the product across all stores.
   - Fill missing Delivery_Time using the mode of the delivery time for each region.

2. **Outlier Detection:**
   - Identify outliers in Sales_Qty by checking values outside the range of ± 2 standard deviations from the mean for each store.

3. **Standardize Date Format:**
   - Convert all Date values to a consistent format (e.g., YYYY-MM-DD).

4. **Categorical Encoding:**
   - Convert the Region variable to numeric codes (North = 1, South = 2, East = 3).

Preprocessed Data:

Store_ID	Product_ID	Sales_Qty	Stock_Level	Delivery_Time (days)	Date	Region	Sales_Qty_Filled	Stock_Level_Filled	Delivery_Time_Filled
S001	P001	120	50	5	2024-01-01	North	120	50	5
S002	P002	80	30	7	2024-01-02	South	80	30	7
S001	P003	110	40	4	2024-01-03	North	110	40	4
S003	P001	150	60	5	2024-01-04	East	150	60	5
S002	P002	90	25	6	2024-01-05	South	90	25	6
S001	P001	110	50	5	2024-01-06	North	110	50	5
S003	P003	130	45	3	2024-01-07	East	130	45	3

Output and Results:

1. **Sales Quantity Missing Data**:
   o The missing sales quantity for S001-P003 was filled with the median of the available sales values for the same product across other stores (110 units).

2. **Stock Level Missing Data**:
   o The missing stock level for S001-P001 was filled with the average stock level of 50 for that product across all stores.

3. **Delivery Time Missing Data**:

- o The missing delivery time for S003-P001 was filled with the most frequent delivery time (5 days) in the East region.

4. **Outliers**:

- o No outliers detected for Sales_Qty based on the standard deviation range (since all values fall within the ±2 standard deviation range from the mean).

5. **Categorical Data Transformation**:

- o The region values (North, South, East) were converted to numerical codes: North = 1, South = 2, East = 3.

Observations:

- **Missing Data**: Missing values in Sales_Qty, Stock_Level, and Delivery_Time were filled effectively using median, mean, and mode imputation strategies, making the dataset more complete and reliable.

- **Consistency**: The date format was standardized, making it easier to perform time-based analyses.

- **Outliers**: No outliers were found, which indicates that sales quantities were fairly consistent within normal operational ranges.

- **Regional Analysis**: The encoding of regions allows for easier analysis and integration with other machine learning models or analytical tools.

Decisions from the Supply Chain Management Perspective:

- **Inventory Management**: The filling of missing stock levels ensures that inventory management systems can make decisions based on full data, reducing the risk of stockouts or excess inventory.

- **Demand Forecasting**: With the cleaned sales data, demand forecasting models can now be applied more accurately, as the missing values are no longer a problem.

- **Supply Chain Optimization**: The consistent and clean dataset allows for better optimization of supply chain activities, such as ordering, replenishment, and delivery scheduling, as it can now handle real-time data for more precise forecasting and planning.

Conclusion:

Data preprocessing is a critical step in supply chain analytics. By addressing missing values, standardizing data formats, and eliminating outliers, the dataset becomes more reliable and ready for further analysis, leading to more informed decisions and improved efficiency in supply chain management.

4.1 Data Cleaning and Transformation

Data cleaning and transformation are crucial steps in the data preparation process, ensuring that the data is accurate, consistent, and in a suitable format for analysis. The first step in cleaning data typically involves identifying and handling missing values. Missing data can occur for a variety of reasons, such as errors in data entry or incomplete information. These gaps need to be addressed, either by filling in the missing values using estimation techniques, such as imputation, or by removing incomplete records, depending on the analysis requirements and the importance of the data.

Next, inconsistencies within the data must be addressed. This involves checking for and correcting any errors in data entries, such as misspellings, incorrect values, or formatting issues. For instance, dates may be entered in different formats, or numerical values may be recorded with varying units. Standardizing these values ensures uniformity across the dataset, making it easier to analyze and compare. This step also includes removing duplicate entries that can distort results.

Data transformation is equally important, as it ensures the data is in a form that is both suitable for analysis and aligns with the needs of the specific models or methods being used. This process can involve various tasks, such as normalizing numerical data to ensure that all variables are on the same scale or converting categorical data into numerical form through encoding techniques. The goal is to make the dataset more accessible and interpretable, especially when applying machine learning algorithms or statistical models that require specific data formats.

One aspect of data transformation is feature engineering, where new variables or features are created from the existing ones. This can involve aggregating data, such as calculating averages or totals, or deriving new metrics that provide additional insights. Feature engineering plays a critical role in improving the performance of machine learning models by providing more relevant and informative input. It can also help reduce the complexity of the data by simplifying it into a smaller set of more meaningful variables.

Another key element in data cleaning and transformation is data integration. Often, data comes from multiple sources, and combining these datasets into a single, cohesive set is essential for a comprehensive analysis. This may involve matching records across different tables, handling discrepancies between sources, or resolving conflicts in data values. Proper data integration ensures that the final dataset reflects all the necessary information and is free from inconsistencies that could arise from disparate data sources.

Finally, once the data has been cleaned and transformed, it is important to validate it to ensure its integrity and suitability for analysis. This involves checking for outliers, verifying the accuracy of transformations, and confirming that the dataset meets the requirements of the analysis or model. Validation helps to identify any lingering issues that might affect the outcomes of data analysis, ensuring that the final dataset is both reliable and actionable for decision-making.

Practical Example Context: Cleaning Inconsistent Product Data for Demand Forecasting in a Wholesale Business

In a wholesale business, demand forecasting relies heavily on historical sales data, which is often inconsistent due to human errors, data entry issues, or system mismatches. For instance, a product might be recorded with inconsistent names, missing prices, or incorrect quantities. Cleaning this data is essential to ensure accurate demand forecasting. In this example, we'll focus on cleaning inconsistent product data for a better understanding of how data quality influences forecasting outcomes.

Sample Data Before Cleaning

Product ID	Product Name	Category	Sales Quantity	Price per Unit	Date
P001	Apple	Fruit	120	0.5	2024-01-01
P002	Banana	Fruit	150	0.3	2024-01-01
P003	apple (green)	Fruit	100	0.55	2024-01-02
P004	Orange	Fruit	180	0.6	2024-01-02
P001	Apple (green)	Fruit	130	0.5	2024-01-03
P005	Grapes (seedless)	Fruit	200	1.0	2024-01-02

Product ID	Product Name	Category	Sales Quantity	Price per Unit	Date
P003	Apple	Fruit	110	0.55	2024-01-03
P002	Banana (yellow)	Fruit	160	0.3	2024-01-03
P001	Apple	Fruit	0	0.5	2024-01-04
P006	Pear	Fruit	130	0.7	2024-01-01

- Load the Data into a data analysis software / tool
- Analyze the data.

Steps for Cleaning:

1. **Standardize Product Names**: Ensure all products with similar names are unified (e.g., "apple" and "apple (green)" should be the same).

2. **Handle Missing Data**: Identify and fill in any missing sales data, or exclude rows where data is incomplete.

3. **Check for Duplicate Entries**: Remove duplicates or aggregate sales data where the same product appears multiple times for the same period.

4. **Correct Price Inconsistencies**: Check for pricing errors and align the price per unit for the same products.

Cleaned Data

Product ID	Product Name	Category	Sales Quantity	Price per Unit	Date
P001	Apple	Fruit	250	0.5	2024-01-01

Product ID	Product Name	Category	Sales Quantity	Price per Unit	Date
P002	Banana	Fruit	310	0.3	2024-01-01
P003	Apple	Fruit	210	0.55	2024-01-02
P004	Orange	Fruit	180	0.6	2024-01-02
P005	Grapes (seedless)	Fruit	200	1.0	2024-01-02
P006	Pear	Fruit	130	0.7	2024-01-01

Explanation and Interpretation of Results

- **Standardization**: The product names are unified (e.g., "apple (green)" and "apple" are now consistent). This ensures that the demand forecast will treat all sales of apples (green or not) as one unified product.

- **Aggregated Sales Data**: Duplicate entries for products on different dates were consolidated to get accurate sales quantities (e.g., P001's sales quantities across different dates were aggregated).

- **Missing Sales Data**: Missing sales entries for some products were filled where possible (e.g., P001's zero sales on 2024-01-04 could be attributed to a data entry error, hence it was removed from forecasting).

Observations

1. **Product Sales Consolidation**: The cleaning process reveals the true total sales for each product. For instance, "Apple" had 250 units sold over multiple days, rather than separate, misleading data points.

2. **Consistency in Product Names**: Standardizing product names reduces forecasting confusion, ensuring that future demand predictions are not diluted by inconsistent naming conventions.

3. **Accurate Price per Unit**: Price is now standardized for consistent pricing, ensuring accurate profitability calculations during forecasting.

Decisions from a Supply Chain Management Perspective

1. **Improved Forecasting Accuracy**: By cleaning the data, the forecast will be more accurate, enabling better inventory planning and demand predictions.

2. **Inventory Optimization**: With cleaner data, the business can avoid overstocking or understocking products. For instance, by knowing the true demand for "Apple," the company can order the right amount to meet the expected demand.

3. **Supplier Coordination**: Accurate product and sales data allow better communication with suppliers, improving lead times and reducing stockouts.

4. **Demand Fluctuations**: The cleaned data helps in identifying trends in demand that were previously obscured by inconsistent reporting (e.g., whether a surge in sales for bananas is seasonal or promotional).

By maintaining clean and accurate data, the business can make more informed, strategic decisions that ultimately drive operational efficiency and cost savings.

4.2 Handling Missing and Outlier Data

Handling missing and outlier data is a crucial aspect of data preprocessing, as both can significantly affect the accuracy of analysis or model performance. Missing data occurs when some values are not recorded or are absent due to various reasons such as errors during data collection or technical issues. It can lead to biased or misleading conclusions if not addressed properly. There are several ways to handle missing data, with the most common methods being deletion, imputation, or using algorithms that can handle missing values naturally. Deletion involves removing rows or columns with missing values, which is simple but can result in the loss of valuable information. Imputation fills in missing values based on other available data, such as replacing them with the mean, median, mode, or more complex methods like using machine learning models to predict missing values.

Outliers, on the other hand, are values that significantly differ from other observations and can distort the analysis if not treated properly. These outliers may occur due to errors in data collection, recording mistakes, or they could be genuinely rare but valid values. Identifying outliers is often done by statistical methods, such as visual inspection of data plots like boxplots or histograms, or by using mathematical techniques such as the Z-score. Once identified, outliers can be handled in various ways, depending on the context. They can be removed if they are deemed to be errors or irrelevant to the analysis, or they can be adjusted or transformed to reduce their impact.

In some cases, instead of removing or modifying outliers, data scientists might choose to keep them if they represent valuable, rare events, such as fraudulent transactions in a financial dataset. However, it's essential to thoroughly understand the context of the data before making such decisions. Additionally, outliers can sometimes indicate interesting phenomena or the presence of unique patterns, so discarding them without careful analysis can lead to the loss of potentially important insights.

The impact of missing data and outliers can also depend on the type of data and the specific analysis being performed. For instance, missing data in a time-series dataset could create gaps that affect trends, whereas outliers in a classification problem might distort the decision boundary between classes. Consequently, the methods for handling missing values and outliers should be selected with consideration of the overall goal of the analysis and the type of algorithm being used. In predictive modeling, many machine learning algorithms are sensitive to both missing data and outliers, which is why addressing these issues before model training is essential.

There are no one-size-fits-all solutions for missing data and outliers, so it's important to experiment with different strategies and evaluate their impact. For instance, trying out various imputation techniques, such as mean imputation, regression imputation, or even k-nearest neighbors imputation, can yield different results depending on the dataset. Similarly, the decision of whether to remove or transform outliers depends on the problem at hand. In some cases, robust models such as decision trees or random forests may perform well even with outliers present, whereas linear models might require more careful treatment of these data points.

Ultimately, the goal is to ensure that the data is in a form that allows for accurate and reliable analysis. By properly handling missing values and outliers, data scientists can improve the quality of the dataset, which in turn leads to more trustworthy and actionable insights. This process is an essential part of the data cleaning and preprocessing phase, which lays the foundation for any successful data analysis or machine learning task. Careful consideration of how to deal with these issues ensures that the results of any model or analysis are both robust and interpretable.

Practical Example: Imputing Missing Sales Data and Detecting Outliers in Customer Orders

A retail company has customer order data that tracks product sales across multiple regions. However, some sales data is missing, and there are anomalies such as unusually high or low sales numbers that could be outliers. The goal is to fill in the missing sales data using imputation techniques and detect outliers to ensure that the data used for forecasting and decision-making is clean and reliable.

Sample Data:

Order ID	Customer ID	Product ID	Sales Quantity	Region	Date
1	C001	P101	50	North	2025-01-01
2	C002	P102	20	South	2025-01-02

Order ID	Customer ID	Product ID	Sales Quantity	Region	Date
3	C003	P101	NULL	East	2025-01-03
4	C004	P103	300	West	2025-01-04
5	C005	P102	40	North	2025-01-05
6	C001	P101	50	North	2025-01-06
7	C006	P104	100	South	2025-01-07
8	C007	P103	200	East	2025-01-08
9	C002	P102	5000	North	2025-01-09
10	C005	P101	30	West	2025-01-10

- Load the Data into a data analysis software / tool
- Analyze the data.

Steps:

1. **Impute Missing Sales Data:**

   We can fill the missing value for Order ID 3 using mean imputation for Product P101, which is the average sales quantity for Product P101 across all other orders.

   - Mean sales quantity for P101: (50 + 50 + 30) / 3 = 43.33.
   - Imputed value for Order ID 3: 43.33.

2. **Detect Outliers:**

Using the **Z-score method** (considering values greater than 3 or less than -3 as outliers):

- ○ Z-score = (X - mean) / standard deviation
- ○ We can calculate the Z-scores for each product's sales quantities and identify outliers.

Updated Table After Imputation:

Order ID	Customer ID	Product ID	Sales Quantity	Region	Date	Z-Score	Is Outlier
1	C001	P101	50	North	2025-01-01	0.27	No
2	C002	P102	20	South	2025-01-02	-0.88	No
3	C003	P101	43.33	East	2025-01-03	0	No
4	C004	P103	300	West	2025-01-04	0.58	No
5	C005	P102	40	North	2025-01-05	0.12	No
6	C001	P101	50	North	2025-01-06	0.27	No
7	C006	P104	100	South	2025-01-07	-0.58	No
8	C007	P103	200	East	2025-01-08	-0.19	No
9	C002	P102	5000	North	2025-01-09	4.43	Yes
10	C005	P101	30	West	2025-01-10	-0.76	No

Interpretation and Observations:

- **Imputation Result:** The missing sales value for Order ID 3 has been imputed as 43.33 based on the average sales quantity for Product P101, ensuring that the data is complete and ready for analysis.

- **Outlier Detection:**

  - The sales quantity of 5000 units for Product P102 (Order ID 9) is flagged as an outlier with a Z-score of 4.43, which is significantly higher than typical sales values.

  - All other entries fall within the expected range, with Z-scores indicating no significant deviations.

Supply Chain Management Perspective:

1. **Imputation of Missing Data:** The imputation helps ensure that the data is consistent and complete, which is critical for accurate demand forecasting, inventory management, and reporting.

2. **Outlier Detection and Action:**

   - The outlier of 5000 units for Product P102 could indicate an error, such as a data entry mistake, or it could reflect an unusually large order (e.g., a bulk purchase or promotional event).

   - The supply chain team should investigate the cause of this anomaly. If it was a data error, correcting it will prevent incorrect demand forecasts. If it was a legitimate large order, adjusting the supply chain forecast to account for this kind of variability might be needed.

3. **Impact on Forecasting:** Imputation and outlier detection help ensure that the data used for demand forecasting and inventory management is accurate, reducing the risk of stockouts or overstock situations.

4. **Inventory Replenishment:** Identifying outliers allows for better adjustment in inventory management. A huge order like the one in Order ID 9 might require an immediate replenishment, while smaller fluctuations are handled by the standard inventory system

4.3 Feature Engineering for Supply Chain Applications

Feature engineering in supply chain applications involves the process of selecting, modifying, or creating new input features from raw data to improve the performance of machine learning models. This process is essential because it helps transform the raw data into a format that algorithms can better understand, leading to more accurate predictions and decision-making. For instance, supply chain data might include transactional information, product details, delivery schedules, and supplier performance. By carefully choosing the right features, businesses can gain insights into operational efficiencies, demand forecasting, inventory optimization, and cost reduction.

One key area of feature engineering in supply chain management is demand forecasting. Predicting future demand for products accurately is crucial for managing inventory levels and ensuring timely delivery. Features such as historical sales data, seasonality, promotional activities, and external factors like weather or holidays can all contribute to more accurate forecasts. By engineering features that capture trends and patterns in historical data, businesses can improve their ability to predict demand fluctuations and respond accordingly.

Another important application of feature engineering is in the optimization of inventory management. Data related to stock levels, order frequency, supplier lead times, and product shelf life are just a few examples of features that can be extracted or transformed to help improve inventory control. For example, features that highlight the age of inventory or trends in product movement over time can aid in decision-making related to reorder points, stock rotation, and product discontinuation. This helps minimize stockouts and reduce excess inventory, improving cash flow and operational efficiency.

In supply chain logistics, feature engineering can play a critical role in route optimization and transportation management. Key features might include delivery times, transportation costs, vehicle capacity, traffic conditions, and geographical locations. By crafting features that take into account factors like time of day, route preferences, and vehicle performance, businesses can create more efficient delivery schedules and reduce fuel consumption, thereby cutting costs and improving service levels.

Supplier performance is another area where feature engineering can significantly impact supply chain operations. Features such as lead time variability, quality of goods, historical performance metrics, and supplier reliability can help organizations evaluate and select suppliers more effectively. By identifying patterns in supplier performance over time, businesses can reduce the risks associated with delays or quality issues, improving overall supply chain resilience and customer satisfaction.

Lastly, feature engineering also plays a role in the broader strategic decisions of a supply chain, such as risk management and sustainability. By incorporating features that reflect environmental impact, supply chain disruptions, or geopolitical factors, businesses can better assess the risks associated with different suppliers, transportation routes, and inventory strategies. This enables proactive decision-making that not only addresses operational challenges but also aligns with sustainability goals and market expectations.

Practical Example: Creating Features for Lead Time Prediction Using Historical Shipping Data

A company in the retail industry wants to predict lead times for shipments from suppliers to its warehouses in order to optimize inventory levels and improve order fulfillment efficiency. The historical shipping data from the past 12 months is used to create features for a lead time prediction model. The company tracks various variables such as order date, shipment date, shipping method, distance between the supplier and the warehouse, and the size of the order.

Sample Data (Shipping Data for 5 Orders)

Order ID	Order Date	Shipment Date	Shipping Method	Distance (km)	Order Size (units)	Lead Time (days)
001	2024-01-10	2024-01-12	Air Freight	500	100	2
002	2024-02-05	2024-02-08	Ground Freight	300	200	3
003	2024-03-01	2024-03-03	Air Freight	400	150	2
004	2024-03-20	2024-03-22	Sea Freight	2000	500	2

Order ID	Order Date	Shipment Date	Shipping Method	Distance (km)	Order Size (units)	Lead Time (days)
005	2024-04-10	2024-04-15	Ground Freight	800	100	5

- Load the Data into a data analysis software / tool

- Analyze the data.

Features for Lead Time Prediction

1. **Order Date**: The date the order was placed.

2. **Shipping Method**: Mode of shipment (e.g., air, ground, sea).

3. **Distance**: Distance between the supplier and the warehouse (in kilometers).

4. **Order Size**: Number of units ordered.

5. **Day of the Week**: Day of the week when the order was placed (could influence processing time).

Output: Predicted Lead Time Using Machine Learning Model (e.g., Random Forest)

Order ID	Predicted Lead Time (days)	Actual Lead Time (days)	Error (days)
001	2	2	0
002	3	3	0
003	2	2	0
004	3	2	1
005	4	5	-1

Explanation and Interpretation of Results:

- **Model Accuracy**: The prediction model accurately predicts lead times for most orders, with the exception of Order ID 004, where the predicted lead time was off by 1 day. In this case, sea freight, which typically has longer lead times, was underestimated.

- **Error Analysis**: The error for Order ID 005 was -1 day, meaning the model predicted a shorter lead time than the actual lead time, which could be due to delays that weren't captured in the features.

- **Feature Impact**: Distance and shipping method are significant predictors of lead time, as seen in the table. Orders with longer distances (e.g., Order 004 with sea freight) tend to have higher lead times.

Observations:

1. **Shipping Method**: Air freight has the shortest lead times, followed by ground and sea freight. Sea freight tends to introduce a higher variability in lead time, as seen in the prediction error for Order 004.

2. **Order Size**: While the model does not explicitly show this in the results, larger orders may lead to longer handling times, though the current data does not strongly reflect this pattern in predicted vs. actual lead time.

3. **Distance**: Longer shipping distances lead to longer lead times, with air and ground methods still performing consistently better over shorter distances.

Supply Chain Management Decisions:

1. **Inventory Optimization**: With accurate lead time predictions, the company can optimize inventory levels at the warehouse, reducing stockouts and excess inventory.

2. **Shipping Method Choices**: The company can use the prediction model to decide when to prioritize faster shipping methods, particularly for high-demand products or time-sensitive orders.

3. **Supplier Relationships**: If certain suppliers consistently have longer or more variable lead times, negotiations can focus on improving their performance or adjusting the forecasted delivery windows to avoid stockouts.

4. **Operational Efficiency**: The model can help identify inefficiencies in the supply chain, particularly for longer-distance shipments, enabling the company to explore alternative routes or logistics providers for better performance.

This data-driven approach can help improve supply chain reliability, reduce costs, and increase customer satisfaction by aligning inventory levels more closely with expected lead times.

5. Predictive Analytics in Supply Chain

Predictive analytics in supply chain management refers to the use of data, statistical algorithms, and machine learning techniques to forecast future events and trends. It allows businesses to anticipate demand, identify potential disruptions, and optimize various processes like inventory management, procurement, and logistics. By leveraging historical data, companies can make more informed decisions, minimize risks, and improve efficiency. Predictive analytics helps companies stay ahead of market fluctuations, reducing the chances of stockouts or overstocking, and ultimately ensuring a smoother flow of goods.

One of the key areas where predictive analytics can make a significant impact is demand forecasting. By analyzing past sales data, seasonality, market trends, and external factors, companies can predict future customer demand with greater accuracy. This enables businesses to adjust production schedules, plan for required raw materials, and ensure sufficient stock levels, all while minimizing waste. Accurate demand forecasting also aids in reducing lead times and optimizing warehouse space, improving overall supply chain efficiency.

Another critical application of predictive analytics is in the identification and management of risks. Supply chains are often subject to disruptions caused by natural disasters, geopolitical events, supplier issues, or transportation delays. Predictive models can analyze a wide range of variables to forecast potential risks and help companies prepare contingency plans. This proactive approach allows businesses to mitigate the impact of disruptions by adjusting operations, finding alternative suppliers, or rerouting shipments before issues arise.

Predictive analytics also plays a vital role in inventory management. By understanding future demand patterns and product lifecycles, companies can optimize stock levels across multiple locations, reducing the cost of holding inventory while ensuring they have enough products available to meet customer needs. This results in improved cash flow, better customer satisfaction, and fewer stockouts or excess inventory. Moreover, predictive models can indicate which products are likely to become obsolete, helping companies avoid over-investing in items that won't sell.

Transportation and logistics are also enhanced through predictive analytics. By forecasting traffic patterns, weather conditions, or potential delays, companies can better plan shipping routes and delivery schedules. This helps in minimizing transportation costs, improving delivery reliability, and ensuring goods reach their destination on time. Predictive models can also identify underperforming routes, enabling logistics managers to optimize fleet usage and reduce fuel consumption.

Finally, predictive analytics enables supply chain visibility, allowing companies to track and monitor operations more effectively. By continuously analyzing data from various sources, such as suppliers, warehouses, and transportation networks, businesses can gain real-time insights into their supply chain performance. This enhanced visibility leads to quicker decision-making and the ability to address issues as they arise, further enhancing the resilience and agility of the supply chain. Ultimately, predictive analytics empowers companies to create more efficient, adaptive, and cost-effective supply chains.

Example Context: Predictive Analytics in Supply Chain

A company wants to predict demand for its products during the upcoming holiday season to optimize inventory and reduce stockouts. They use predictive analytics to forecast demand based on historical sales data and external factors such as market trends, promotional activities, and economic conditions. The dataset contains weekly sales figures for the last year, and the company wants to predict the demand for the next four weeks.

Sample Data

Week	Product A Sales	Product B Sales	Promotional Activity (1 = Yes, 0 = No)	Economic Indicator (Scale 1-10)
1	200	150	1	7
2	180	160	0	6
3	210	180	1	8
4	220	170	1	7
5	230	190	0	6
6	250	200	1	9
7	240	210	1	8
8	230	205	0	7
9	260	220	1	9

Week	Product A Sales	Product B Sales	Promotional Activity (1 = Yes, 0 = No)	Economic Indicator (Scale 1-10)
10	250	215	0	6

- Load the Data into a data analysis software / tool
- Analyze the data.

Output and Results (Predicted Demand for Weeks 11-14)

Week	Predicted Demand for Product A	Predicted Demand for Product B
11	275	230
12	265	225
13	280	235
14	270	220

Interpretation of Results

1. **Demand Forecasting**: The predicted demand for both Product A and Product B is expected to increase in the upcoming weeks, consistent with seasonal trends and previous promotional activities. The increase in sales for both products suggests that the holiday season is driving demand.

2. **Influence of External Factors**: We can see that higher sales tend to correlate with periods of economic improvement (higher economic indicators) and promotional activities. For example, in Week 6, where both promotional activity and a high economic indicator were present, sales spiked for both products.

3. **Seasonality Impact**: The demand for both products is expected to rise steadily, which aligns with the company's anticipation of a busy holiday season.

Observations

1. **Promotion Effects**: Promotional activities seem to have a significant impact on the demand for both products. Weeks with

promotions show higher sales figures compared to non-promotion weeks. Therefore, promotions should be strategically planned to align with demand spikes.

2. **Economic Indicator Correlation**: Sales also appear to be influenced by the economic environment, with weeks of higher economic indicators showing better sales performance. Thus, the company should monitor economic trends and adjust its supply chain strategy accordingly.

3. **Predictive Accuracy**: The forecast aligns with past trends, but external shocks (e.g., market changes, weather, or geopolitical factors) could affect future results. A more complex model (e.g., including weather data) could improve accuracy.

Decisions from the Supply Chain Management Perspective

1. **Inventory Planning**: The company should prepare for higher demand by increasing inventory in advance of weeks 11–14, particularly for Product A, which shows a larger increase in forecasted demand.

2. **Stock Replenishment Strategy**: The supply chain team should coordinate with suppliers to ensure there is enough stock on hand to meet the anticipated demand spikes. This may include negotiating faster delivery times or increasing orders for high-demand products.

3. **Promotion Scheduling**: Since promotions significantly boost sales, the company should consider running additional promotional campaigns during the forecasted demand peaks, especially for Product B, which has more consistent growth patterns.

4. **Risk Mitigation**: Given the reliance on external economic factors, the company should develop contingency plans to account for potential disruptions, such as supply chain delays or a sudden downturn in the economy.

5.1 Forecasting Demand with Time Series Models

Demand forecasting is a crucial aspect of business operations, helping companies predict future demand for their products or services. One of the most reliable methods for demand forecasting is time series modeling, which focuses on analyzing historical data to identify patterns and trends that can be used to predict future values. Time series models are particularly useful because they account for the sequential nature of data, where past observations often influence future events. These models make it possible to plan resources effectively, optimize inventory, and adjust production schedules based on expected demand.

The key advantage of time series models is their ability to capture trends, seasonality, and other underlying patterns in the data. Trends refer to long-term movements in demand, such as an increase or decrease over time. Seasonality represents periodic fluctuations, such as higher demand during the holiday season or specific months of the year. Understanding these patterns is essential for making accurate forecasts, as businesses can anticipate regular changes in demand and prepare accordingly.

In a time series model, past demand values are typically used to predict future values. This historical data might include daily, weekly, monthly, or yearly records, depending on the specific context. By examining past data, businesses can identify cycles and patterns that reoccur, helping them make predictions about upcoming demand. For instance, if a product consistently experiences higher demand during the summer months, the time series model will recognize this seasonality and adjust forecasts to reflect the seasonal peak.

The choice of model depends on the complexity of the demand pattern and the business's forecasting needs. Some simple time series models, like moving averages or exponential smoothing, may suffice for businesses with relatively stable demand. More sophisticated models, such as autoregressive integrated moving average (ARIMA), are used when the data exhibits more complex patterns. These models take into account both recent and past observations to make predictions about future demand, allowing businesses to refine their forecasts as new data becomes available.

Time series forecasting also benefits from the incorporation of external factors, which can influence demand but are not necessarily part of the historical data set. For example, economic indicators, weather patterns, or promotional campaigns can all have a significant impact on demand. While traditional time series models focus primarily on the internal data, modern techniques often integrate these external factors to improve forecast accuracy. Incorporating such variables requires a more advanced understanding of the relationship between these external influences and the demand patterns.

Despite their power, time series models are not infallible, and businesses must continuously evaluate and adjust their forecasting methods. Forecast accuracy can be impacted by changes in the underlying patterns, such as shifts in consumer behavior, market conditions, or external events like natural disasters or global pandemics. To maintain accuracy, time series models require regular updates and recalibration to ensure they reflect current trends. As a result, businesses should use these models as part of a broader forecasting strategy that includes ongoing monitoring and adaptation to emerging conditions.

Practical Example: Demand Forecasting for a Grocery Store Chain Using ARIMA Models

A grocery store chain wants to forecast the weekly demand for a popular product (e.g., organic milk) across its various locations. By accurately predicting future demand, the store can optimize inventory, reduce stockouts, and minimize overstocking. The ARIMA (AutoRegressive Integrated Moving Average) model is used for this time series forecasting based on historical sales data.

Sample Data (Weekly Sales for 10 Weeks):

Week	Sales (Units)
1	120
2	135
3	140
4	130
5	145
6	150
7	160
8	170
9	175

Week	Sales (Units)
10	180

- Load the Data into a data analysis software / tool

- Analyze the data.

Step 1: Apply ARIMA Model

The ARIMA model requires three components:

- **p (AR)**: The number of lag observations included in the model (AutoRegressive term).

- **d (I)**: The number of times the series needs to be differenced to achieve stationarity (Integrated term).

- **q (MA)**: The size of the moving average window (Moving Average term).

After analyzing the data and checking for stationarity, the model parameters are set as follows:

- **p = 1** (based on ACF/PACF plots indicating that past week's demand is a good predictor of future demand).

- **d = 1** (due to slight trend, we use first differencing).

- **q = 1** (because of the moving average structure observed in the residuals).

Step 2: Forecast Future Sales for the Next 4 Weeks

Week	Actual Sales (Units)	Forecast Sales (ARIMA Model)	Forecast Error
1	120		
2	135		
3	140		
4	130		
5	145		

Week	Actual Sales (Units)	Forecast Sales (ARIMA Model)	Forecast Error
6	150		
7	160		
8	170		
9	175		
10	180		
11		185	
12		190	
13		195	
14		200	

Step 3: Interpretation of Results

- The ARIMA model forecasts a steady increase in sales, reflecting a trend observed in the historical data. For instance, week 11 is expected to see 185 units sold, continuing the upward trend.

- **Forecast Error**: A key metric in demand forecasting is the forecast error. This can be calculated as the difference between actual sales and forecast sales once the actual data is available. Here, the forecasted values for weeks 11–14 are estimates, and their accuracy will be determined once actual sales are recorded.

Observations

- The ARIMA model accurately reflects the general trend in the data, with increasing demand in each subsequent week.

- Short-term fluctuations and seasonal patterns might not be perfectly captured since this is a simple ARIMA model without additional components like seasonality or exogenous variables.

- The forecast error will be critical in adjusting future predictions, as the model may need refinement if actual sales deviate significantly from the forecasts.

Decisions from the Supply Chain Management Perspective

1. **Inventory Planning**: The forecasted demand provides key information for inventory replenishment. The store can order approximately 185 units of organic milk for week 11, adjusting for any lead time.

2. **Safety Stock**: Based on the forecast error and historical demand variability, the store may maintain safety stock to account for unexpected demand surges or supply disruptions.

3. **Promotions & Discounts**: If sales are forecasted to rise, marketing might plan promotions to capitalize on increased demand. On the other hand, if forecasts show lower-than-expected sales, discounts might be used to drive consumption.

4. **Supply Chain Coordination**: The forecast allows better alignment with suppliers, ensuring timely delivery of goods. Suppliers can adjust production schedules based on the forecasted demand, reducing the risk of stockouts.

5. **Cost Management**: By minimizing overstocking, the store can reduce costs associated with storage and spoilage of perishable items, and by avoiding stockouts, it ensures customer satisfaction, improving sales performance.

5.2 Predicting Transportation and Supply Chain Disruptions

Transportation and supply chain disruptions are increasingly unpredictable due to various global and local factors. Natural disasters, such as hurricanes, floods, or wildfires, can significantly impact key infrastructure like roads, ports, and railways. When these events occur in critical supply chain hubs, they can cause delays and shortages in the delivery of goods. While these disruptions are often sudden, their impact can be long-lasting, especially if recovery efforts are slow or complicated by logistical bottlenecks or labor shortages.

Another critical factor influencing transportation disruptions is geopolitical instability. Trade wars, tariffs, and even political unrest can interrupt the flow of goods between countries, affecting global supply chains. For example, a country imposing tariffs or sanctions on another can disrupt the movement of key materials, forcing companies to seek alternative routes or suppliers, which can lead to delays and higher costs. Similarly, political protests or civil unrest can disrupt transportation routes, especially in areas where roads or ports are critical to both local and international trade.

Technological disruptions also play a significant role in transportation and supply chain delays. The rise of cyber-attacks targeting logistics companies or transportation networks can cripple operations. Hackers may disable systems that manage inventory, shipment tracking, or even physical transportation mechanisms. When these systems go down, it may take days or weeks for companies to regain control, which can halt the movement of goods and even lead to security concerns over sensitive cargo. As companies increasingly rely on automation and digital tools, vulnerabilities in these technologies present new risks.

Labor shortages also contribute significantly to supply chain disruptions. Many industries depend heavily on truck drivers, warehouse workers, and port staff to keep the movement of goods smooth. When these workers are in short supply due to retirements, illness, or insufficient training, transportation networks slow down, resulting in longer wait times and increased costs. Moreover, strikes or labor disputes can escalate disruptions, especially when key labor forces in transport hubs or warehouses are involved.

Global pandemics like COVID-19 have shown the fragility of supply chains. The pandemic highlighted how a sudden and widespread health crisis can lead to labor shortages, factory shutdowns, and transportation bottlenecks. While the world has started to recover, ongoing health risks or future pandemics could again disrupt global networks. Even when economies return to normal, the lingering effects on transportation schedules and inventory levels can persist for months, causing ripples throughout the system.

Finally, environmental concerns and regulatory changes are increasingly affecting supply chains. The push toward sustainability has led to the introduction of stricter regulations on emissions and the types of transportation vehicles that can be used. Compliance with these regulations can add delays or costs, especially if companies need to upgrade their fleets or adjust their logistics practices to meet new standards. Environmental regulations can also affect the availability of certain materials or restrict transportation routes, especially in regions that prioritize conservation efforts or biodiversity protection. These evolving regulatory environments can complicate forecasting and planning, increasing the likelihood of unanticipated disruptions.

Practical Example: Predicting Transportation Delays Using Weather and Traffic Data

A logistics company is interested in predicting transportation delays for their delivery routes. The company uses weather and traffic data to predict potential delays on various routes. To achieve this, they analyze historical data from weather forecasts, traffic patterns, and delivery times to build a predictive model.

Sample Data

Let's assume the company has gathered historical data for five delivery routes and the associated weather and traffic conditions for the past week.

Date	Route	Weather Condition	Traffic Density	Delivery Time (hrs)	Actual Delay (hrs)
2025-01-01	A	Clear	Low	2.5	0
2025-01-01	B	Rainy	High	3.5	1.5
2025-01-02	A	Snow	Medium	3.0	1.0

Date	Route	Weather Condition	Traffic Density	Delivery Time (hrs)	Actual Delay (hrs)
2025-01-02	C	Clear	Low	1.5	0
2025-01-03	B	Rainy	High	4.0	2.0
2025-01-03	D	Fog	Medium	2.0	0.5
2025-01-04	C	Clear	Low	2.0	0
2025-01-04	D	Snow	High	3.0	1.5

- Load the Data into a data analysis software / tool

- Analyze the data.

Predicted Delays using Weather and Traffic Data:

To predict transportation delays, the model considers **weather condition** (Clear, Rainy, Snow, Fog), **traffic density** (Low, Medium, High), and **historical delivery times**. The model uses this information to predict potential delays in hours for the upcoming deliveries.

Predicted Delay Results:

Date	Route	Predicted Delay (hrs)
2025-01-01	A	0
2025-01-01	B	1.6
2025-01-02	A	0.9
2025-01-02	C	0
2025-01-03	B	2.1
2025-01-03	D	0.7

Date	Route	Predicted Delay (hrs)
2025-01-04	C	0
2025-01-04	D	1.6

Explanation and Interpretation of Results:

1. **Weather Influence**: Routes with snow or rain (like Route B and D) tend to have higher delays (predicted delay of 1.6–2.1 hours). This is due to the decreased visibility and road conditions that disrupt the flow of traffic.

2. **Traffic Influence**: High traffic density generally causes longer delays. For example, on 2025-01-01, Route B experienced high traffic and rain, leading to a predicted delay of 1.6 hours. Even with similar weather, lower traffic densities (like Route A and C) resulted in minimal delays (0–0.9 hours).

3. **Predictions vs. Actual Delays**: On 2025-01-01, Route B had an actual delay of 1.5 hours, and the model predicted 1.6 hours, showing a strong predictive capability. On other dates, the model's predictions were reasonably close to actual delays, although some routes (like Route C) had zero delays but were predicted to have minor delays (0.7 hours for Route D).

Observations:

- **Weather and traffic conditions are significant drivers of delays**, but they may not fully account for real-world complexity, as demonstrated by the occasional discrepancies in predictions.

- The model is more accurate in predicting delays when both **high traffic** and **poor weather conditions** are present (as seen on Routes B and D).

- There is a **potential need for more granular data**—for example, integrating real-time traffic data, road closures, and accidents might improve the model's accuracy.

Supply Chain Management Perspective:

From a **Supply Chain Management (SCM)** perspective, the predictions help in making more informed decisions:

1. **Route Optimization**: The company can prioritize routes with fewer expected delays or choose alternate routes during high-traffic or adverse weather conditions.

2. **Delivery Time Buffering**: Knowing the predicted delays, the logistics team can plan deliveries with appropriate time buffers to avoid disruptions and meet customer expectations.

3. **Resource Allocation**: For high-delay routes, the company may decide to allocate more resources (e.g., additional trucks or drivers) to ensure timely deliveries.

4. **Cost Optimization**: By predicting delays, the company can proactively manage the costs associated with delays (fuel, overtime, and penalties) and avoid potential losses.

The predictive model helps the company to **reduce uncertainty, increase efficiency**, and improve **customer satisfaction** by managing the transportation process more effectively.

5.3 Machine Learning Algorithms for Predictive Analysis

Machine learning algorithms are powerful tools used in predictive analysis to forecast future trends, behaviors, or outcomes based on historical data. These algorithms allow computers to recognize patterns within data and make predictions or decisions without explicit programming for each specific case. At the core of predictive analysis, the primary goal is to use past observations to make educated guesses about what will happen next in similar situations. By learning from large datasets, machine learning models can adapt and improve over time as they encounter more data, making them incredibly valuable in fields ranging from finance and healthcare to marketing and retail.

Supervised learning is one of the most common approaches in predictive analysis, where the algorithm is trained on labeled data. In this type of learning, both the input data and the correct output are provided, allowing the algorithm to learn the mapping between the two. After training, the model can be used to predict outcomes for new, unseen data based on the patterns it has learned. This method is commonly used for regression tasks, where the goal is to predict a continuous value, or classification tasks, where the goal is to assign an input to one of several categories.

Another approach is unsupervised learning, where the model works with unlabeled data. Unlike supervised learning, the algorithm doesn't have access to the correct answers but tries to discover hidden patterns or structures within the data on its own. Unsupervised learning is often used for clustering, where the algorithm groups similar data points together, or dimensionality reduction, where the goal is to reduce the number of variables to make the data easier to analyze without losing important information.

There are also semi-supervised learning techniques, which combine elements of both supervised and unsupervised learning. These algorithms are used when only a small portion of the data is labeled, and the rest is unlabeled. The model initially trains on the labeled data and then uses the structure found in the unlabeled data to refine its predictions. This approach is useful when acquiring labeled data is expensive or time-consuming, but large amounts of unlabeled data are available.

Reinforcement learning is another type of machine learning that is especially useful in situations where the algorithm needs to make a series of decisions over time, such as in robotics or game-playing. In reinforcement learning, the algorithm learns by interacting with its environment and receiving feedback in the form of rewards or penalties based on its actions. Over time, it seeks to maximize its cumulative reward, learning the best strategies or behaviors to achieve a desired goal.

The accuracy and effectiveness of machine learning models in predictive analysis depend largely on the quality and quantity of the data used for training, as well as the choice of algorithm. Some algorithms, like decision trees and neural networks, are well-suited to certain types of problems, while others, like support vector machines or k-nearest neighbors, may perform better in different contexts. Additionally, the ability to fine-tune the parameters and adjust for overfitting or underfitting is crucial in ensuring that the model generalizes well to new, unseen data, which is ultimately the goal of predictive analysis.

Practical Example Context:

A retail company wants to predict potential product stockouts for a specific product category based on historical sales and inventory data. The company is using a Random Forest algorithm to forecast stockouts for a product (e.g., "Product X") at different store locations. The input features include past sales data, inventory levels, promotions, and lead time, and the goal is to predict whether a stockout will occur in the upcoming week.

Sample Data:

Week	Store Location	Sales	Inventory Level	Lead Time (days)	Promotion (1 = Yes, 0 = No)	Stockout (1 = Yes, 0 = No)
1	Store A	120	30	3	0	0
2	Store A	150	20	2	1	1
3	Store A	130	15	5	0	1
4	Store A	100	25	4	0	0
5	Store B	80	40	3	0	0
6	Store B	110	18	2	1	1
7	Store B	90	10	4	0	1

Week	Store Location	Sales	Inventory Level	Lead Time (days)	Promotion (1 = Yes, 0 = No)	Stockout (1 = Yes, 0 = No)
8	Store B	70	35	3	0	0
9	Store C	200	50	1	1	0
10	Store C	210	30	2	0	0
11	Store C	220	20	3	1	1
12	Store C	150	15	2	0	1

- Load the Data into a data analysis software / tool
- Analyze the data.

Random Forest Model Output:

After training the Random Forest model on the historical data, the algorithm outputs predictions for stockouts. Let's assume that the model predicts stockouts for weeks 2, 3, 6, 7, and 11 for Store A, Store B, and Store C.

Week	Store Location	Predicted Stockout (1 = Yes, 0 = No)	Actual Stockout (1 = Yes, 0 = No)
1	Store A	0	0
2	Store A	1	1
3	Store A	1	1
4	Store A	0	0
5	Store B	0	0
6	Store B	1	1
7	Store B	1	1
8	Store B	0	0
9	Store C	0	0

Week	Store Location	Predicted Stockout (1 = Yes, 0 = No)	Actual Stockout (1 = Yes, 0 = No)
10	Store C	0	0
11	Store C	1	1
12	Store C	0	1

Explanation and Interpretation:

- **Accuracy:** Out of 12 weeks, the model correctly predicted stockouts in 10 cases (weeks 2, 3, 6, 7, and 11), yielding an accuracy rate of 83.3%. It was incorrect only for week 12, where it predicted no stockout, but there was one (False Negative).

- **True Positives (TP):** The model correctly predicted stockouts in weeks 2, 3, 6, 7, and 11. This means that in these weeks, the prediction aligns with the actual events.

- **False Positives (FP):** The model predicted stockouts in weeks 1, 4, 5, 8, and 9 where there was no stockout. These are false alarms that may lead to unnecessary actions like restocking, which could incur additional costs.

- **False Negatives (FN):** The model failed to predict a stockout in week 12, where a stockout did occur. This indicates a missed opportunity to mitigate the stockout by timely restocking.

Observations:

1. **Promotion Impact:** In weeks with promotions (weeks 2, 3, 6, 7, and 11), the model seems to predict stockouts more frequently. Promotions often boost demand, making stockouts more likely, which the model recognizes.

2. **Sales and Inventory Levels:** The model appears to use historical sales data and inventory levels to predict stockouts effectively. Weeks with low inventory levels and higher sales often lead to predicted stockouts (weeks 3, 6, and 7).

3. **Lead Time:** The model uses lead time as a feature, but it is not always the determining factor. For example, week 3 had a 5-day lead time but still experienced a stockout despite a longer lead time.

Decisions from a Supply Chain Management Perspective:

1. **Restocking Strategy:** The company should focus on increasing the stock levels in weeks when sales surge, especially during promotions, to reduce the chances of stockouts. Proactive restocking based on predictions can help ensure sufficient inventory during high-demand periods.

2. **Inventory Replenishment Policies:** Establish an automated restocking policy that triggers earlier when stockout risk is high (based on Random Forest predictions). This minimizes stockouts and ensures products are available when customers need them.

3. **Promotional Planning:** Given the correlation between promotions and stockouts, the company may want to refine its promotional strategies to align better with inventory management practices.

4. **Review False Negatives:** The company should investigate why stockouts were missed in week 12, where the model predicted no stockout. Possible factors could include delayed data updates or unknown seasonal effects not captured by the model.

5.4 Demand Sensing and Stock Replenishment in Warehousing

Demand sensing refers to the process of using real-time data to understand and anticipate customer demand more accurately. In warehousing, this involves the integration of various data sources, such as sales, market trends, and even social media signals, to gain insights into shifts in consumer preferences or buying patterns. By capturing this information early, warehouses can adjust their operations accordingly, helping to prevent stockouts or overstock situations that could disrupt the supply chain.

Stock replenishment is a critical part of warehouse management, ensuring that inventory levels are maintained at optimal levels to meet customer demand. Without adequate stock replenishment strategies, warehouses may face inefficiencies, including excess inventory that ties up capital or insufficient stock that leads to missed sales opportunities. The goal of stock replenishment is to align the amount of stock on hand with the anticipated demand, which is where demand sensing plays a key role.

With accurate demand sensing, warehouses can make better decisions about when and how much to reorder. For example, if demand signals indicate an uptick in sales for a particular product, a warehouse can trigger stock replenishment to avoid running out of inventory. Conversely, if demand is predicted to drop, the warehouse can reduce the replenishment order, avoiding the need for excess storage or markdowns.

The integration of demand sensing and stock replenishment systems also helps to improve operational efficiency. By utilizing advanced forecasting tools and real-time data analytics, warehouses can minimize waste, reduce lead times, and enhance order fulfillment. This responsiveness ensures that stock levels are always aligned with demand, ultimately leading to cost savings and improved customer satisfaction.

Additionally, the use of automation and machine learning in both demand sensing and stock replenishment can further optimize warehouse operations. Automated systems can help identify patterns in historical data and adapt to new trends faster than traditional methods. As these systems become more sophisticated, they can predict future demand with increasing accuracy, enabling warehouses to stay ahead of shifts in the market.

In the competitive landscape of warehousing, demand sensing and stock replenishment are no longer optional; they are essential components of a modern supply chain strategy. Companies that can effectively sense demand

and adjust their stock levels accordingly gain a significant advantage in meeting customer needs, reducing operational costs, and maintaining supply chain agility. Through continuous monitoring and optimization, warehouses can achieve a more efficient and responsive system that adapts to ever-changing market dynamics.

Practical Example:

A retail warehouse is using machine learning to optimize replenishment schedules for a selection of products based on historical sales data. The goal is to reduce stockouts, optimize inventory levels, and improve order fulfillment by predicting demand more accurately. The warehouse utilizes data from previous sales over the last 12 months to forecast demand for the upcoming quarter. Based on this forecast, the replenishment schedule will be adjusted to maintain optimal stock levels for each product category.

Sample Data:

Product ID	Product Name	Sales (Jan - Mar)	Sales (Apr - Jun)	Sales (Jul - Sep)	Sales (Oct - Dec)	Total Sales	Average Monthly Sales	ML Forecasted Demand (Next Quarter)	Replenishment Order
101	Widget A	500	600	550	580	2230	557	600	600
102	Gadget B	300	350	400	380	1430	357	375	375
103	Tool C	150	120	180	200	650	162	175	175
104	Component D	200	250	220	230	900	225	225	225
105	Accessory E	450	420	460	440	1770	442	450	450

- Load the Data into a data analysis software / tool

- Analyze the data.

Output and Results Interpretation:

- **Average Monthly Sales**: The table includes the total sales across four quarters for each product, with the average monthly sales calculated. For example, **Widget A** has an average of 557 units sold per month.

- **Machine Learning Forecasted Demand**: This column indicates the machine learning model's predicted demand for the next quarter. For example, the ML forecast for **Widget A** is 600 units. This is based on seasonality, trends, and patterns identified in the past sales data.

- **Replenishment Order**: This column shows the recommended replenishment quantity for each product. For **Widget A**, the order quantity is 600 units, which is aligned with the forecasted demand.

Observations:

1. **Stock Level Alignment**: The replenishment orders generally align with the forecasted demand. For example, **Gadget B** has an average of 357 units sold per month and is forecasted to need 375 units for the next quarter. This slight increase in demand is accounted for, likely due to a seasonal surge or trend.

2. **Product-Specific Variations**: The forecast for **Tool C** shows a lower demand of 175 units compared to its average monthly sales of 162 units, indicating that the product may experience increased demand in the upcoming quarter.

3. **Adjustments for Variability**: Products like **Widget A** and **Accessory E** show stable and relatively predictable demand patterns, whereas **Tool C** shows more variability. This could reflect seasonality or external market factors impacting sales.

Supply Chain Management Decisions:

1. **Inventory Optimization**: The recommended replenishment quantities are optimized based on the forecast, helping to minimize stockouts while avoiding overstock. For example, **Gadget B**'s forecast of 375 units ensures that it has enough stock for the next quarter while avoiding excessive inventory.

2. **Supply Chain Coordination**: The replenishment order reflects the accuracy of demand forecasting, leading to better coordination between suppliers and the warehouse. Products like **Tool C** might

need closer monitoring to ensure that any changes in demand are quickly reflected in future forecasts.

3. **Seasonal Adjustments**: The replenishment strategy should consider seasonality. For example, if **Widget A** is a highly seasonal product, adjustments may be needed to reflect higher demand during a peak season, especially in the second quarter.

4. **Cost Efficiency**: Accurate forecasts reduce unnecessary stock levels, optimizing storage costs. If the replenishment order for **Tool C** is too high, the warehouse might incur higher holding costs. Ensuring that the order quantity aligns with actual demand will minimize wasted resources.

By applying machine learning to sales data, the warehouse can better align inventory levels with demand, reduce waste, and improve customer satisfaction through better availability of products.

6. Optimization in Supply Chain Decision Making

Optimization in supply chain decision-making refers to the process of making the best possible decisions to enhance the efficiency and effectiveness of the entire supply chain. It involves identifying the most effective ways to manage resources, streamline operations, and satisfy customer demands while minimizing costs. The aim is to create a system that responds quickly to changes in demand, supply conditions, and other market dynamics, ensuring that products are available where and when they are needed, with minimal waste or excess inventory.

One key aspect of optimization is the balancing of supply and demand. In supply chains, demand can fluctuate due to various factors, including seasonality, economic conditions, or unexpected events. By using optimization techniques, companies can predict these changes and adjust their supply strategies to prevent stockouts or overstocking. Proper forecasting helps in planning production schedules, inventory management, and distribution, allowing businesses to meet customer expectations while minimizing excess inventory that ties up capital.

Another area of focus is transportation and logistics. Optimizing transportation routes, scheduling deliveries, and selecting the right carriers can significantly reduce costs and improve service levels. By evaluating factors like fuel efficiency, delivery times, and transportation mode selection, companies can cut down on unnecessary costs. Advanced technologies, such as route optimization algorithms, help businesses minimize delays and ensure timely delivery, which is critical for maintaining customer satisfaction in competitive markets.

Inventory management is also crucial in optimizing supply chain decisions. Companies must ensure they hold just enough stock to meet demand without overstocking, which can lead to higher holding costs. Optimization models help determine the right levels of inventory at various stages of the supply chain. These models take into account lead times, demand variability, and the costs associated with carrying inventory, helping to strike the right balance between having enough stock and not overburdening the business with excess inventory.

Supplier relationships and procurement strategies also play a significant role in supply chain optimization. By selecting the right suppliers, negotiating favorable terms, and maintaining strong partnerships, businesses can improve both cost efficiency and the reliability of their supply chains. Optimization techniques can help in evaluating suppliers based on performance metrics like cost, quality, and lead time, ensuring that the company chooses the best suppliers for its needs while fostering long-term, mutually beneficial relationships.

Finally, integrating technology into supply chain operations has made optimization more accessible and effective. Tools such as enterprise resource planning (ERP) systems, artificial intelligence, machine learning, and real-time tracking allow businesses to collect vast amounts of data. This data can be analyzed to identify inefficiencies, predict disruptions, and inform decision-making processes. The use of advanced analytics and automation in decision-making has transformed supply chain management, enabling companies to optimize operations dynamically and respond quickly to changes in the market.

Practical Example:

A company manufactures and distributes products across three regional warehouses, aiming to minimize total costs (including transportation, inventory holding, and ordering costs). The company needs to determine the optimal order quantities from the central warehouse to each regional warehouse to minimize costs while meeting the demand at each location. The costs vary based on the distance between the central warehouse and regional warehouses, as well as the inventory holding costs.

Sample Data:

Region	Demand (units)	Cost per Unit	Transportation Cost ($/unit)	Holding Cost ($/unit/month)	Order Quantity (units)
North	500	20	5	1.5	450
South	600	22	6	1.3	550
East	400	21	4	1.2	370
West	300	23	7	1.7	280

- Load the Data into a data analysis software / tool
- Analyze the data.

Optimization Output:

Region	Demand (units)	Order Quantity (units)	Transportation Cost ($)	Holding Cost ($)	Total Cost ($)
North	500	450	5 * 450 = 2250	1.5 * 450 = 675	2925
South	600	550	6 * 550 = 3300	1.3 * 550 = 715	4015
East	400	370	4 * 370 = 1480	1.2 * 370 = 444	1924
West	300	280	7 * 280 = 1960	1.7 * 280 = 476	2436

Explanation & Interpretation of Results:

The order quantities reflect an optimization where the company minimizes total costs across transportation and holding expenses. The costs are broken down as follows:

1. **Transportation Costs**: The transportation cost is higher for regions further away (e.g., the West region incurs a $7/unit transportation cost, while the East only has $4/unit).

2. **Holding Costs**: The holding cost is also calculated based on the order quantity and the respective unit holding cost for each region. Holding costs tend to increase with higher order quantities, although the impact varies depending on the unit holding cost (e.g., the West region has a higher holding cost due to a $1.7/unit charge).

3. **Total Cost**: The total cost is the sum of transportation and holding costs. The South region has the highest total cost, despite having a relatively lower transportation cost than the West, due to its higher demand and order quantity.

Observations:

- The **East region** is the most cost-efficient, with the lowest total cost of $1,924 due to a lower transportation cost and reasonable order quantity.

- The **West region**, although closer in demand to the North region, incurs a higher total cost because of both high transportation and holding costs.

- **South region** incurs the highest total cost due to both relatively higher demand and a high transportation cost.

Supply Chain Management Decisions:

1. **Demand-Supply Alignment**: The company might consider revising order quantities, especially for regions like the West and South, to reduce total costs by balancing transportation and holding costs more effectively.

2. **Location Decisions**: The company may want to investigate whether opening additional warehouses or consolidating certain regions would optimize transportation costs further.

3. **Cost Reduction Strategies**: Negotiating with suppliers or transportation partners could potentially lower transportation and holding costs, leading to a more cost-efficient supply chain overall.

By focusing on these optimizations, the company can lower its supply chain costs while maintaining service levels.

6.1 Linear and Integer Programming for Supply Chains

Linear and integer programming are powerful mathematical optimization techniques often applied in supply chain management to solve complex problems related to resource allocation, transportation, production planning, and inventory management. These methods are designed to help businesses maximize or minimize specific objectives, such as cost or time, while adhering to various constraints, such as production capacity or delivery deadlines. Linear programming focuses on problems where decision variables can take any real values, while integer programming is used when these variables are restricted to integer values, which is crucial for decisions that involve discrete items, like the number of trucks or batches.

In supply chain management, linear programming is commonly used for problems like optimizing the transportation of goods from warehouses to retailers. The goal is typically to minimize transportation costs while ensuring that demand at each retail location is met and that transportation capacities are not exceeded. Constraints in these models might include the availability of trucks, storage limits, or production schedules. By creating a model that balances supply and demand with minimal cost, businesses can ensure smoother operations and better resource utilization.

Integer programming is particularly useful in supply chains when decisions are discrete in nature, such as determining the number of trucks to deploy or how many units of a product to produce. In this case, the decision variables must be integers because fractional quantities would not make sense in the context (e.g., a truck cannot be split into a fraction of a vehicle). This method allows companies to deal with real-world scenarios like warehouse selection, vehicle routing, and workforce scheduling, where the decision points are naturally whole numbers.

One of the main advantages of using linear and integer programming in supply chain management is that they allow for optimal solutions. These solutions provide decision-makers with clear guidelines for resource allocation, thereby improving efficiency and reducing costs. Furthermore, they can account for a wide range of constraints, including capacity limits, minimum and maximum requirements, and time windows, ensuring that the solution is both practical and implementable in real-world operations.

However, solving these types of problems can sometimes be computationally intensive, especially when the problem size is large or the number of constraints is high. Integer programming, in particular, tends to be more difficult to solve than linear programming because of the discrete nature of the decision variables. This can lead to longer solution times or require specialized algorithms, like branch-and-bound or branch-and-cut methods, to find the optimal solution.

Despite the complexity, the use of linear and integer programming in supply chains is essential for businesses aiming to stay competitive in an increasingly globalized market. By leveraging these techniques, companies can improve operational efficiency, reduce waste, and ensure that they are meeting customer demand in the most cost-effective way. Whether applied to inventory management, distribution networks, or production scheduling, linear and integer programming help businesses navigate the complexity of modern supply chains and make informed, data-driven decisions.

Practical Example: Optimizing Warehouse Location with Linear Programming

A company wants to minimize the total cost of storing products at different warehouse locations while meeting customer demand across various regions. The company operates three potential warehouse sites (A, B, and C) and serves customers in five regions (1 to 5). The costs of storing products at each warehouse vary, as do the transportation costs from each warehouse to each customer region. The goal is to determine how many products should be stored at each warehouse and which regions each warehouse should supply to minimize the total cost.

Sample Data (Costs in USD)

Warehouse	Storage Cost per Unit	Transportation Cost to Regions (1-5)
A	3	2, 4, 6, 8, 7
B	4	3, 5, 7, 5, 6
C	5	1, 2, 3, 4, 6

Region	Demand (Units)
1	100
2	150

Region	Demand (Units)
3	200
4	120
5	180

- Load the Data into a data analysis software / tool
- Analyze the data.

Objective:

Minimize the total cost, which consists of storage and transportation costs.

Formulation of the Linear Programming Problem

1. **Decision Variables**:

Let x_{ij} be the number of units stored at warehouse i (where i $\in A, B, Ci \in \{A, B, C\}i \in A, B, C)$ for region j.

2. **Objective Function**:

Minimize:

$$Z = \sum i = \sum_{i=1}^{3} \sum_{j=1}^{5} \left(\text{Storage cost}_i + \text{Transportation cost}_{ij} \right)$$

Constraints:

- Demand constraints for each region: $\sum_{i=1}^{3} x_{ij} = \text{Demand}_{ij}$
- $Non - negativity constraints: xij \geq 0 for all i, j$

Linear Programming Output

Assuming the optimization model is solved using an LP solver, the output might look like the following:

Warehouse	Region 1	Region 2	Region 3	Region 4	Region 5	Total Storage Units	Total Cost (USD)
A	60	40	0	0	0	100	1,100
B	40	110	200	120	0	470	2,500
C	0	0	0	0	180	180	1,150
Total	100	150	200	120	180	1,000	4,750

Explanation and Interpretation of Results

- **Warehouse A**: Supplies 60 units to Region 1, 40 units to Region 2, and has a storage cost of $1,100. Since it is cheaper for A to supply regions 1 and 2, it focuses on these regions.

- **Warehouse B**: Supplies most of the units (40 to Region 1, 110 to Region 2, and 200 to Region 3) and incurs a storage and transportation cost of $2,500. B is the most flexible warehouse due to its lower transportation costs to many regions.

- **Warehouse C**: Supplies only Region 5, delivering 180 units, resulting in a total cost of $1,150. C is the most expensive to operate but serves a specific region due to its proximity to Region 5.

Observations and Decisions from a Supply Chain Management Perspective

1. **Cost Distribution**: Warehouse B bears the largest share of the total cost (52.6% of total cost) because it serves the highest demand and multiple regions. Although it is not the cheapest warehouse for storage, its transportation costs balance out, making it the most efficient in this scenario.

2. **Warehouse Selection**: Warehouses A and C have more limited roles but are strategically placed to minimize costs where possible. A serves regions 1 and 2 because of its lower storage cost, while C serves only Region 5, which might indicate a geographic advantage.

3. **Demand Fulfillment**: The model ensures all customer demand is met while optimizing costs. Regions with higher demand are primarily served by Warehouse B due to its proximity to many regions.

Supply Chain Decisions:

- **Warehouse Location Strategy**: If the company wants to optimize for cost, it should continue to invest in Warehouse B, which plays a central role in fulfilling multiple regions' demands at a lower overall cost. Warehouse A and C should be used strategically for specific regions where they offer cost advantages.

- **Transportation and Storage Cost Management**: The company should focus on reducing transportation costs for Warehouse B, as it handles a large volume of demand. If possible, it could invest in regional distribution centers or explore alternate transportation modes to further reduce costs.

- **Future Adjustments**: The company could explore expanding Warehouse A's capacity or improving transportation infrastructure to reduce reliance on Warehouse B in the future.

This linear programming model provides a data-driven approach to warehouse location decisions, ensuring the company can make cost-effective choices in its supply chain.

6.2 Network Design and Optimization

Network design and optimization involve the process of planning and configuring a network to meet specific performance and reliability requirements. The goal is to create an efficient system that can handle the expected traffic loads while minimizing costs and maintaining high-quality service. In designing a network, it's important to consider the type of services the network will support, the geographical location of users, and the hardware and software available. An effective network design ensures that resources such as bandwidth, routers, and servers are optimally allocated to achieve the desired outcome.

Optimization is crucial for improving the performance of an existing network. Once a network is designed and implemented, it's necessary to evaluate how well it's functioning and identify areas that need improvement. Optimization techniques may include reducing latency, increasing bandwidth, and improving data routing efficiency. The goal is to fine-tune the network so that it operates as smoothly and quickly as possible, even as traffic patterns change or new services are introduced.

Traffic management is a key aspect of network optimization. Networks often experience varying levels of traffic depending on the time of day, user demand, or special events. A well-designed network accounts for peak times and ensures that the system can still function effectively under heavy load. Techniques like load balancing, traffic shaping, and congestion management are used to distribute traffic evenly across the network, preventing bottlenecks and maintaining high performance.

Another aspect of optimization is security. A network must be secure from potential threats such as data breaches, malware, and denial-of-service attacks. Security measures can be implemented during the design phase to ensure that there are appropriate firewalls, encryption methods, and access controls in place. Continuous monitoring and updates are also crucial to detect and mitigate potential vulnerabilities over time. A network that is not optimized for security can leave critical systems exposed to various risks.

Scalability is an essential consideration in both design and optimization. As user demand grows or as new technologies emerge, a network must be able to scale without major disruptions. This requires designing the network to be flexible, with enough capacity to handle future expansions. Additionally, optimization helps ensure that as the network grows, its performance remains stable, and the increased load doesn't lead to inefficiencies or slowdowns. The ability to scale seamlessly is a key indicator of a well-optimized network.

Finally, regular monitoring and maintenance play an important role in both network design and optimization. Even the best-designed networks need ongoing attention to ensure they continue to meet performance standards. Monitoring tools can track metrics such as latency, throughput, and error rates, providing valuable insights into the network's health. This allows administrators to address problems before they become significant issues. Optimizing a network is a continuous process that requires constant attention to evolving needs and technologies.

Practical Example:

A new retailer, FastTrends, is looking to design an optimal distribution network for its retail outlets. The company intends to minimize transportation costs while ensuring timely delivery of products to the stores. The company has identified three potential distribution centers (DCs) located in different regions and wants to evaluate the most cost-effective distribution strategy. The primary factors to consider are the transportation cost per unit between DCs and retail outlets, the demand at each store, and the warehouse capacity of each DC.

Sample Data:

Retail Store	Demand (units)	DC1 Distance (miles)	DC2 Distance (miles)	DC3 Distance (miles)	Transportation Cost per Unit ($)	DC1 Capacity (units)	DC2 Capacity (units)	DC3 Capacity (units)
Store A	500	150	300	450	2	1000	800	1200
Store B	300	200	250	350	2.5	1000	800	1200
Store C	700	400	350	250	3	1000	800	1200

- Load the Data into a data analysis software / tool

- Analyze the data.

Objective:

Minimize transportation costs by assigning stores to distribution centers based on demand and distance.

Output Results:

Store	Assigned DC	Units Supplied	Distance (miles)	Transportation Cost ($)	Total Transportation Cost ($)
Store A	DC1	500	150	1000	1000
Store B	DC2	300	250	750	750
Store C	DC3	700	250	2100	2100
Total					4850

Explanation and Interpretation:

- **Store Assignments**: Each store is assigned to the DC that minimizes the transportation cost based on the distance and cost per unit. Store A is assigned to DC1, Store B to DC2, and Store C to DC3.

- **Transportation Costs**: For each store, the transportation cost is calculated as Demand * Transportation Cost per Unit * Distance. For example, Store A's cost is 500 * 2 * 150 = 1000.

- **Total Transportation Cost**: The total cost for fulfilling the demand at all stores is the sum of individual transportation costs, resulting in **$4850**.

Observations:

1. **Distance Factor**: The closer DCs (DC1 for Store A) result in lower transportation costs, which directly affects the overall logistics expenses.

2. **Demand Matching**: Matching higher demand stores with more centrally located DCs (DC3 for Store C) can further optimize costs.

3. **Capacity Considerations**: All stores' demand is within the capacity limits of their assigned DCs, ensuring no overloading.

Decisions from the Supply Chain Management Perspective:

1. **Optimal Distribution Network**: Based on the analysis, the retailer should proceed with this distribution network setup, as it minimizes transportation costs.

2. **Future Expansion Considerations**: The company should evaluate whether the current DCs can handle growth in demand and how changes in distance (due to new store openings) might affect costs.

3. **Cost Reduction Strategies**: The retailer could explore consolidating shipments or negotiating lower transportation rates for long-distance deliveries, further reducing costs.

This example highlights the importance of data-driven decision-making in supply chain design to achieve cost efficiency and meet service levels.

6.3 Inventory Management Optimization Techniques

Inventory management optimization focuses on striking the right balance between having enough stock to meet customer demand and not overstocking, which can lead to excess costs. One effective technique is to implement just-in-time (JIT) inventory. This approach reduces inventory holding costs by ensuring that products arrive as they are needed for production or sale. Companies relying on JIT closely monitor supplier performance and delivery times to minimize delays, making the process efficient and reducing waste.

Another technique involves demand forecasting. Accurate predictions of future sales help businesses plan inventory more effectively. By analyzing historical data, market trends, and seasonality, companies can ensure they have enough stock without over-purchasing. Tools like predictive analytics and machine learning models can help refine these forecasts, allowing businesses to react to shifting customer preferences or unexpected disruptions more swiftly.

Centralized inventory management is another optimization strategy. It involves consolidating inventory in one location or a few strategic sites, reducing the need for multiple smaller warehouses. This makes it easier to track stock levels, reduce duplication, and minimize the risk of stockouts. However, this requires an efficient and reliable transportation network to ensure that inventory is delivered promptly to meet demand at various locations.

Technology plays a crucial role in streamlining inventory management. Automation tools and advanced software systems can track stock levels, order trends, and even reorder supplies when thresholds are met. Real-time data updates and integration with other business functions, like sales and purchasing, create a seamless process that improves decision-making and reduces human errors. Additionally, RFID and barcode scanning technology can improve accuracy in stocktaking and reduce the likelihood of discrepancies.

Supplier relationship management also contributes to better inventory optimization. By maintaining strong, transparent relationships with suppliers, companies can negotiate better terms, ensure faster deliveries, and reduce lead times. Building reliable partnerships with suppliers also provides more flexibility in handling sudden demand changes or supply chain disruptions, allowing for more agile inventory management.

Finally, regularly reviewing and adjusting inventory policies based on performance and market changes is crucial. This involves assessing stock levels, turnover rates, and sales patterns, ensuring that inventory strategies remain aligned with the company's evolving needs. Businesses that regularly audit and adjust their processes can stay ahead of potential inefficiencies and better manage their cash flow while providing customers with the right products at the right time.

Practical Example: Optimizing Stock Levels and Replenishment Strategies for a Retail Chain

Sample Data:

Store	Product	Current Stock	Average Weekly Demand (units)	Lead Time (days)	Safety Stock (units)	Replenishment Order (units)
A	P1	50	30	7	20	40
A	P2	80	60	10	30	90
A	P3	40	20	5	15	25
B	P1	60	35	7	22	45
B	P2	90	50	9	28	75
B	P3	30	15	6	12	20
C	P1	70	40	8	25	50
C	P2	85	55	7	27	65
C	P3	50	30	5	18	40

- Load the Data into a data analysis software / tool

- Analyze the data.

Replenishment Strategy:

- **Safety Stock:** A buffer to prevent stockouts, considering lead time variability.

- **Replenishment Order:** The number of units to order based on current stock, average demand, and safety stock.

The replenishment order can be calculated using the formula:

$$Replenishment\ Order$$
$$= (Average\ Weekly\ Demand \times Lead\ Time\ in\ Weeks)$$
$$- Current\ Stock + Safety\ Stock$$

Output and Results:

Using the formula, we calculate the replenishment orders for each product at each store:

Store	Product	Current Stock	Average Weekly Demand (units)	Lead Time (days)	Safety Stock (units)	Replenishment Order (units)
A	P1	50	30	7	20	40
A	P2	80	60	10	30	90
A	P3	40	20	5	15	25
B	P1	60	35	7	22	45
B	P2	90	50	9	28	75
B	P3	30	15	6	12	20
C	P1	70	40	8	25	50
C	P2	85	55	7	27	65
C	P3	50	30	5	18	40

Interpretation of Results:

- **Product P1**: Stores A, B, and C have relatively similar replenishment orders due to similar demand patterns. Store C has the highest replenishment order (50 units) because of higher safety stock and slightly higher demand.

- **Product P2**: This product has the highest replenishment requirement across all stores, particularly at Store B, where both demand and lead time are high. Store A's replenishment order is also high due to a combination of high demand and lead time.

- **Product P3**: The replenishment orders are generally lower, indicating that demand is moderate and stock levels are more aligned with the sales pace.

Observations:

1. **Higher Replenishment Orders for High-Demand Products**: Products like P2 require larger replenishment orders to meet higher average weekly demand and account for higher safety stock.

2. **Variation Across Stores**: Even though the demand for the same product (e.g., P1) is relatively similar across stores, replenishment orders differ due to safety stock and lead time considerations.

3. **Lead Time Influence**: Lead time plays a significant role in the order calculations. For products with higher lead time, stores must order more inventory upfront to prevent stockouts.

Supply Chain Management Decisions:

1. **Optimal Stock Levels**: Ensure that the safety stock is balanced with the actual demand. Overestimating safety stock could lead to excess inventory, increasing holding costs.

2. **Replenishment Frequency**: Depending on lead time, some stores may need more frequent stock replenishment (especially for products with higher demand and longer lead times).

3. **Supply Chain Collaboration**: Maintain close coordination with suppliers to manage lead times effectively and reduce delays that could disrupt stock levels.

4. **Forecasting Accuracy**: The accuracy of demand forecasting is critical. Incorrect demand estimations could lead to either stockouts (if underestimated) or overstocking (if overestimated).

By continuously refining the replenishment strategy with accurate demand forecasts, optimal safety stock levels, and effective communication across the supply chain, the retail chain can optimize inventory levels, reduce costs, and improve service levels.

7. Machine Learning and Artificial Intelligence in Supply Chain

Machine learning (ML) and artificial intelligence (AI) are increasingly transforming the way supply chains operate, making processes more efficient and responsive. These technologies enable companies to process vast amounts of data and derive insights that were previously difficult or time-consuming to obtain. With AI, supply chain managers can predict demand, optimize routes, and even identify potential disruptions before they happen. By automating routine tasks, AI reduces the chances of human error, speeds up decision-making, and frees up employees to focus on more strategic aspects of the business.

One of the most important applications of AI and ML in supply chains is demand forecasting. Traditional forecasting methods often rely on historical data and intuition, which can be inaccurate in the face of changing market conditions. AI, on the other hand, uses machine learning algorithms to analyze large datasets and identify complex patterns that humans may not easily recognize. This allows businesses to predict demand more accurately and make better decisions about inventory levels, production schedules, and resource allocation.

AI also plays a crucial role in logistics optimization. Machine learning can analyze factors like traffic patterns, weather conditions, and delivery schedules to determine the most efficient routes for transporting goods. This can reduce transportation costs, improve delivery times, and decrease the carbon footprint of supply chain operations. In addition, AI-powered systems can adjust in real-time if there are disruptions, such as road closures or unexpected delays, ensuring that goods are delivered on time and with minimal disruption.

Automation is another key benefit of AI in the supply chain. By automating routine processes, such as order processing, inventory management, and warehouse operations, AI reduces the need for manual intervention. For example, autonomous robots can be used to move goods in a warehouse, while AI-powered systems can automatically restock inventory based on real-time data. This increases efficiency, reduces operational costs, and allows companies to scale their operations more easily without the need to hire additional staff.

AI and machine learning are also enhancing the ability to monitor and manage risks in supply chains. With real-time data collection and analysis, businesses can identify potential issues early, such as supplier delays, quality problems, or geopolitical events that could disrupt operations. AI can even help companies assess the financial stability of suppliers, predict the likelihood of delays, and suggest alternative sources if necessary. This helps supply chain managers make more informed decisions and take proactive measures to mitigate risks.

Finally, the integration of AI and ML in supply chains is paving the way for more sustainable operations. Machine learning models can predict the most energy-efficient production processes and identify areas where waste can be minimized. AI can also help optimize packaging, reduce transportation distances, and improve resource utilization, all of which contribute to a greener supply chain. As sustainability becomes an increasingly important factor for businesses and consumers alike, AI offers valuable tools for reducing the environmental impact of supply chain operations.

Example Context: Predicting Demand in Supply Chain with Machine Learning

In a supply chain, accurate demand forecasting is crucial for inventory management, resource allocation, and minimizing costs. A retail company uses Machine Learning (ML) and Artificial Intelligence (AI) to predict future product demand, allowing for more efficient stock management and minimizing both stockouts and overstock. The company uses historical data like sales figures, weather patterns, and seasonal trends to train a predictive model. The ML algorithm predicts demand for a particular product in the next month.

Sample Data:

Month	Historical Sales (Units)	Weather Index	Promotion (1=Yes, 0=No)
Jan	150	20	0
Feb	180	22	1
Mar	200	25	0
Apr	250	30	1
May	300	35	1
Jun	350	40	0

- Load the Data into a data analysis software / tool

- Analyze the data.

Machine Learning Model Output (Predicted Demand for July - September):

Month	Predicted Demand (Units)	Predicted Error Margin	Confidence Interval
Jul	320	15%	280 - 360
Aug	280	12%	250 - 310
Sep	330	10%	300 - 360

Explanation & Interpretation:

- **Predicted Demand**: This is the forecasted number of units for each month based on the historical data and the trained machine learning model.

- **Predicted Error Margin**: The model predicts demand with a certain margin of error, which shows the expected variability around the forecast. A 15% error margin in July means the actual demand could vary by up to 15% more or less than the forecasted demand.

- **Confidence Interval**: This provides the range in which the actual demand is likely to fall, based on the model's confidence. For instance, in July, demand is predicted to be between 280 and 360 units, giving the supply chain team a range for planning.

Observations:

1. **Seasonality**: The demand increases significantly from January to June, suggesting seasonal fluctuations (e.g., summer promotions).

2. **Promotions Impact**: Months with promotions (Feb, Apr, May) show higher sales, indicating that marketing activities affect demand.

3. **Prediction Accuracy**: As the error margin decreases from July to September (15% in July down to 10% in September), the model's accuracy is improving, likely due to the system adapting to more stable seasonal patterns.

Decisions from Supply Chain Management Perspective:

- **Inventory Planning**: Given the predicted demand for July to September, the company should begin preparing for higher demand in July and September (330 units), with a safety stock for the upper limit of the confidence interval.

- **Promotions**: Based on the model, promotions are likely to increase demand, so the company should plan for targeted marketing efforts, particularly in July and September.

- **Risk Mitigation**: The predicted error margin highlights the uncertainty in demand forecasting. Supply chain managers should account for the variability (e.g., extra stock or safety stock) to avoid stockouts during the peak months, especially when dealing with a high-demand range.

By leveraging ML and AI for demand forecasting, the company can make more informed decisions, optimize its supply chain operations, and reduce the risk of both overstocking and understocking.

7.1 Supervised vs Unsupervised Learning for Supply Chain

Supervised learning and unsupervised learning are two fundamental approaches in machine learning, each suited for different types of problems in supply chain management. In supervised learning, the algorithm is trained using labeled data, where each input is paired with a correct output. This allows the model to learn a mapping between inputs and outputs. In the context of supply chain, supervised learning can be used for demand forecasting, where historical sales data, along with corresponding demand labels, help the model predict future demand.

On the other hand, unsupervised learning works with unlabeled data, where the algorithm tries to find patterns or relationships without predefined output. In a supply chain scenario, unsupervised learning can be useful for clustering products based on similar characteristics, identifying segments of customers, or detecting anomalies in logistics data. This type of learning can help organizations uncover hidden patterns or outliers that might not be immediately obvious.

One of the main advantages of supervised learning is its ability to produce highly accurate predictions, especially when enough labeled data is available. For example, if a supply chain manager wants to predict the lead time for orders or identify the best suppliers based on past performance, supervised learning can deliver precise insights by learning from past data. However, it requires a large amount of labeled data, which can be time-consuming and expensive to collect.

Unsupervised learning, however, offers more flexibility since it doesn't rely on labeled data. This makes it particularly useful in scenarios where labeled data is scarce or difficult to obtain. It can help supply chain professionals gain a deeper understanding of their operations and customers by exploring patterns and trends that are not immediately apparent. For instance, unsupervised algorithms could segment customers based on purchasing behavior, allowing for more tailored marketing strategies.

The challenge with supervised learning is that it may not adapt well to new or unforeseen situations that weren't part of the training data. If there is a shift in the supply chain, like a new market or disruption, the model might struggle unless retrained with new data. In contrast, unsupervised learning is more robust in dealing with new situations since it's constantly seeking out patterns in the data without a strict reliance on past labels.

In conclusion, the choice between supervised and unsupervised learning in supply chain applications depends largely on the problem at hand. Supervised learning is ideal for tasks requiring accurate predictions based on historical data, while unsupervised learning excels in discovering hidden patterns and organizing data in meaningful ways. By leveraging both techniques, supply chain professionals can improve decision-making, optimize operations, and better understand the dynamics of their networks.

Practical Example: Using Clustering (Unsupervised Learning) for Customer Segmentation in Retail.

In a retail company, customer data is collected to understand purchasing behaviors and segment the customers for targeted marketing and inventory management. The company decides to use unsupervised learning (clustering) to group customers based on similar shopping patterns, which will help improve supply chain decisions, like stock allocation and promotion strategies.

Sample Data (Customer Data):

Customer ID	Age	Annual Income (in $)	Spending Score (1-100)	Product Categories Purchased
1	25	45,000	60	Clothing, Electronics
2	40	90,000	80	Furniture, Electronics
3	22	30,000	30	Grocery, Clothing
4	35	60,000	70	Appliances, Furniture
5	50	100,000	85	Furniture, Electronics, Clothing
6	60	120,000	95	Furniture, Appliances
7	28	55,000	45	Grocery, Clothing
8	38	75,000	65	Electronics, Appliances
9	45	85,000	50	Grocery, Furniture
10	30	50,000	55	Clothing, Electronics

- Load the Data into a data analysis software / tool

- Analyze the data.

Applying Clustering (e.g., K-Means):

- **Clustering Process:**

  Using the K-Means algorithm with k=3 clusters (based on customer spending behavior and income), we perform clustering on the dataset.

- **Cluster Centers (Centroids) after Running K-Means:**

  - **Cluster 1 (Budget Shoppers):** Age = 30, Income = $50,000, Spending Score = 55

  - **Cluster 2 (Mid-Income Shoppers):** Age = 38, Income = $75,000, Spending Score = 65

  - **Cluster 3 (High-Income Shoppers):** Age = 50, Income = $100,000, Spending Score = 80

Output (Clustered Data):

Customer ID	Cluster	Age	Annual Income (in $)	Spending Score (1-100)
1	1	25	45,000	60
2	3	40	90,000	80
3	1	22	30,000	30
4	2	35	60,000	70
5	3	50	100,000	85
6	3	60	120,000	95
7	1	28	55,000	45
8	2	38	75,000	65
9	2	45	85,000	50
10	1	30	50,000	55

Interpretation of Results:

- **Cluster 1 (Budget Shoppers)**: These customers tend to be younger (mid-20s to early 30s) with lower annual incomes (around $45,000), and moderate to low spending scores. Their purchasing behavior likely revolves around essential goods like clothing, electronics, and groceries.

- **Cluster 2 (Mid-Income Shoppers)**: These customers are in their late 30s to early 40s with incomes around $60,000 to $85,000, and have moderate to high spending behavior. They purchase a mix of furniture, electronics, and home appliances, indicating a balance between essential and luxury goods.

- **Cluster 3 (High-Income Shoppers)**: These are older customers (50s and 60s) with significantly higher incomes (above $90,000) and high spending scores. They prefer luxury items like high-end furniture and appliances, which are often long-term investments.

Observations:

- **Customer Segmentation:** The clustering successfully separated the customers into distinct groups based on income and spending behavior.

- **Shopping Patterns:** Budget shoppers tend to buy low-cost and essential items, mid-income shoppers opt for a mix of functional and aspirational products, and high-income shoppers invest in premium products.

Decisions from the Supply Chain Management Perspective:

1. **Inventory Allocation:**
   - **Cluster 1** (Budget Shoppers): Increase stock of affordable products like basic clothing, small electronics, and groceries.
   - **Cluster 2** (Mid-Income Shoppers): Balance stock between affordable home goods (furniture, appliances) and mid-range electronics.
   - **Cluster 3** (High-Income Shoppers): Prioritize luxury and high-end products, ensuring premium appliances and furniture are well-stocked.

2. **Promotional Strategy:**

- Target **Cluster 1** with discounts or promotional offers on essential goods to increase sales.

- Use loyalty programs or product bundles for **Cluster 2** to encourage repeat purchases of high-ticket items.

- For **Cluster 3**, offer exclusive early access to new high-end product lines or premium services to enhance customer loyalty.

3. **Supply Chain Efficiency:**

   - Based on the clusters, optimize the supply chain to reduce stock-outs or overstock situations. For instance, higher-end items for **Cluster 3** may require longer lead times, while essentials for **Cluster 1** should be available with more frequent restocking.

In summary, clustering helps businesses understand their customer base better, enabling more targeted marketing and more efficient supply chain management. By aligning inventory and promotional strategies with customer segments, retail companies can improve sales performance and customer satisfaction.

7.2 Applications of AI in Demand Forecasting

AI plays a significant role in improving the accuracy and efficiency of demand forecasting by leveraging vast amounts of historical data. Through machine learning algorithms, AI can identify patterns and trends that might be too complex for traditional statistical methods to capture. These algorithms can process large datasets quickly, enabling businesses to predict future demand with greater precision. By analyzing past sales, market conditions, and customer behavior, AI can provide more reliable forecasts, which helps companies optimize inventory, reduce costs, and improve customer satisfaction.

One key advantage of AI is its ability to consider multiple variables simultaneously. Traditional methods might focus on a limited set of factors, but AI models can integrate data from a variety of sources, such as weather patterns, social media sentiment, or economic indicators. This comprehensive approach enables businesses to account for a wide range of influences that might affect demand. For example, a sudden change in weather could drive demand for specific products, and AI can adjust predictions accordingly, leading to better inventory management.

Another benefit is AI's ability to continuously learn and adapt over time. As more data becomes available, machine learning models can refine their predictions, improving their accuracy. This dynamic capability is especially important in industries where demand can fluctuate due to unforeseen events, such as supply chain disruptions, economic shifts, or changing consumer preferences. AI systems can also help businesses recognize these shifts early on, providing them with the agility to adjust strategies quickly.

AI can also enhance collaboration across different departments by providing a unified view of demand forecasts. For instance, marketing, sales, and supply chain teams can use the same AI-driven insights to align their strategies. By breaking down silos and enabling more effective communication, AI fosters better decision-making throughout an organization. This holistic approach can lead to more synchronized operations, reducing the risk of overproduction, stockouts, or excess inventory.

Furthermore, AI-driven demand forecasting is particularly useful in industries with complex supply chains or high variability in demand. Retailers, for example, can use AI to predict consumer behavior, helping them stock the right products at the right time. In industries like automotive or electronics, where demand for certain parts or components can be highly unpredictable, AI provides the flexibility to plan and respond more effectively. AI tools can also anticipate potential bottlenecks or disruptions in the supply chain, enabling companies to proactively address issues before they affect demand.

Lastly, AI can help businesses develop more personalized demand forecasts. By analyzing individual customer preferences and behaviors, AI can segment demand at a granular level, predicting what specific products or services certain customers are likely to purchase. This allows companies to fine-tune their inventory and marketing strategies to cater to the needs of different customer groups, resulting in higher customer satisfaction and more efficient resource allocation. Through these applications, AI significantly enhances the accuracy, speed, and adaptability of demand forecasting, providing businesses with a competitive edge in a rapidly changing market environment.

Practical Example: Applying Deep Learning to Predict Demand Fluctuations in Fashion Retail

In the fashion retail industry, predicting demand fluctuations is crucial for managing inventory efficiently and optimizing stock levels. Retailers often face challenges in forecasting demand due to factors like seasonality, trends, and consumer preferences. A deep learning model, specifically a Long Short-Term Memory (LSTM) network, can be employed to predict future demand based on historical sales data. The model uses past sales data, price, promotions, and external factors (like weather or holidays) to make accurate predictions.

Sample Data (Historical Sales Data):

Date	Product Category	Sales Volume	Price ($)	Promotions (%)	Weather (Temp °F)	Holiday (1 = Yes, 0 = No)
2023-01-01	Winter Jacket	150	120	10	32	1
2023-01-02	Winter Jacket	170	115	0	35	0
2023-01-03	Winter Jacket	180	118	5	30	0
2023-01-04	Summer T-shirt	200	25	15	70	0

Date	Product Category	Sales Volume	Price ($)	Promotions (%)	Weather (Temp °F)	Holiday (1 = Yes, 0 = No)
2023-01-05	Summer T-shirt	220	22	10	72	1
2023-01-06	Summer T-shirt	250	20	0	75	0

- Load the Data into a data analysis software / tool
- Analyze the data.

Deep Learning Model Output (LSTM Prediction):

The LSTM model predicts demand for the next 5 days based on the historical data provided:

Date	Predicted Demand (Winter Jacket)	Predicted Demand (Summer T-shirt)
2023-01-07	160	230
2023-01-08	155	240
2023-01-09	170	235
2023-01-10	165	245
2023-01-11	160	250

Explanation & Interpretation of Results:

The model output shows the predicted demand for both Winter Jackets and Summer T-shirts for the next 5 days. For example, for Winter Jackets, the demand is predicted to be around 160 units on 2023-01-07 and is expected to fluctuate between 155 and 170 units for the following days. On the other hand, the Summer T-shirt demand is expected to range from 230 to 250 units, indicating a slight increase in demand with each passing day.

Observations:

1. **Winter Jackets:** The demand for winter jackets is decreasing slightly, which could be due to the approaching end of winter and reduced interest in cold-weather items. The forecast reflects a slight decrease in demand as the temperatures start to rise.

2. **Summer T-shirts:** The demand for summer T-shirts is predicted to increase, which could be attributed to a warmer weather trend and upcoming promotions, especially considering the promotion percentage and the holiday factor in the data. This aligns with the general trend of increased purchases for summer clothing as the season progresses.

3. **Promotions & Holidays:** Promotions and holidays seem to have a positive impact on demand. For example, on 2023-01-05, the promotion of 10% and a holiday (which likely leads to higher consumer activity) led to an increase in sales of Summer T-shirts.

Supply Chain Management Decisions:

1. **Inventory Adjustment:** Based on the forecast, retailers should adjust their inventory for the coming week. Winter jackets may require a reduction in stock to avoid overstocking as demand decreases, while increasing stock for Summer T-shirts to meet the anticipated rise in demand.

2. **Replenishment Strategy:** The supply chain should plan for replenishment cycles for Summer T-shirts, taking into account the projected demand increase. This could involve increasing orders from suppliers to ensure the availability of stock.

3. **Sales & Promotions Strategy:** The model's insights suggest that promotions and holidays boost sales, so the retailer should consider implementing targeted promotions to boost demand, especially during predicted lower-demand periods for Winter Jackets.

4. **Logistics Optimization:** As demand for Summer T-shirts is expected to increase, the supply chain management team might want to ensure that the warehouses have sufficient space and the right logistics partners in place for timely delivery.

In conclusion, deep learning models, when applied to predict demand fluctuations, provide invaluable insights for inventory management and supply chain planning. By leveraging these insights, retailers can make data-driven decisions that align inventory with customer demand, reducing waste and improving sales.

7.3 Reinforcement Learning for Supply Chain Decision Making

Reinforcement Learning (RL) has gained significant attention in recent years for its potential to optimize decision-making processes in various fields, including supply chain management. In a supply chain, decisions must be made about inventory management, production scheduling, order fulfillment, and transportation. These decisions directly impact costs, service levels, and overall operational efficiency. Traditional methods for solving these problems often rely on pre-defined models or heuristics, which may not be flexible enough to adapt to dynamic environments or unexpected disruptions.

RL offers a more flexible approach by allowing systems to learn optimal decision policies through trial and error, based on feedback from the environment. Instead of relying on fixed assumptions, an RL agent interacts with the supply chain environment, making decisions and receiving rewards or penalties based on the outcomes. Over time, the agent learns to improve its decision-making to maximize long-term rewards, which could translate to reduced costs, better service, and increased efficiency.

In the context of inventory management, RL can be used to determine optimal stock levels, order quantities, and reorder points. These decisions are influenced by factors such as demand variability, lead times, and holding costs. An RL agent can adapt its strategy over time by learning from past actions and adjusting to changes in demand or disruptions in supply. This adaptability is a key advantage over traditional methods, which often rely on static forecasts and assumptions.

For production scheduling, RL can help allocate resources efficiently across different production lines or processes, considering constraints such as capacity, labor availability, and machine maintenance schedules. By continuously learning from the outcomes of previous scheduling decisions, an RL agent can find better ways to minimize downtime, reduce bottlenecks, and maximize throughput. The ability to quickly adapt to changes in production conditions is especially valuable in industries where demand and supply fluctuations are common.

Transportation and logistics also benefit from RL applications. Optimizing delivery routes, fleet management, and warehouse operations are complex tasks influenced by numerous variables, including fuel costs, traffic conditions, and delivery windows. An RL agent can learn to navigate these complexities by exploring different strategies and receiving feedback on factors like delivery time and cost. Over time, it can identify more efficient routes and methods for handling logistics, which can lead to significant savings and improved customer satisfaction.

The main advantage of using RL in supply chain decision-making is its ability to learn continuously and adapt to evolving conditions. Unlike traditional methods that require explicit modeling of every possible scenario, RL can handle uncertainty and incomplete information. By leveraging real-time data and iterating on past experiences, RL provides a powerful tool for supply chain managers to make better, more informed decisions that improve performance over the long term. However, implementing RL in a supply chain context can be challenging, as it requires significant computational resources, large amounts of data, and careful consideration of how rewards and penalties are structured to guide learning effectively.

Practical Example: Using Reinforcement Learning to Optimize Dynamic Pricing in a Logistics Company

A logistics company wants to optimize the dynamic pricing of its delivery services to maximize revenue while maintaining customer satisfaction. The company uses Reinforcement Learning (RL) to adjust the prices based on various factors such as demand, distance, package size, delivery urgency, and current market conditions. The RL agent is trained to learn the optimal pricing strategy by interacting with the environment (i.e., receiving customer orders, adjusting prices, and observing outcomes like customer acceptance and delivery efficiency).

Sample Data Table: Dynamic Pricing Optimization Results

Day	Demand (Units)	Base Price (USD)	Price Adjusted by RL (USD)	Revenue (USD)	Customer Acceptance Rate (%)	Delivery Efficiency (%)
1	100	50	55	5500	85	95
2	120	50	52	6240	88	96
3	150	50	60	9000	80	92
4	130	50	57	7410	82	94
5	110	50	53	5830	86	97

Day	Demand (Units)	Base Price (USD)	Price Adjusted by RL (USD)	Revenue (USD)	Customer Acceptance Rate (%)	Delivery Efficiency (%)
6	140	50	58	8120	84	95
7	125	50	56	7000	87	93

- Load the Data into a data analysis software / tool

- Analyze the data.

Explanation and Interpretation of Results:

- **Price Adjustments**: The RL agent adjusts the base price based on demand, customer behavior, and other environmental factors. For example, on Day 3, when demand spikes to 150 units, the price is increased to $60, reflecting a dynamic adjustment to capture more revenue from higher demand.

- **Revenue**: The revenue is maximized on Day 3, where the price adjustment to $60 results in a higher revenue despite a slight drop in customer acceptance. This demonstrates the balance the RL model seeks between price and demand.

- **Customer Acceptance Rate**: As the price increases, customer acceptance generally decreases, as seen on Day 3. However, even with a slight dip in acceptance rate, the overall revenue still increases. This illustrates how RL optimizes pricing to balance the trade-off between customer acquisition and revenue maximization.

- **Delivery Efficiency**: The delivery efficiency remains high throughout the week, ranging from 92% to 97%. The RL agent seems to have optimized the pricing in a way that doesn't negatively impact operational efficiency, which is crucial in logistics.

Observations:

- **Demand-Sensitive Pricing**: The model adjusts prices based on demand, raising the price during high-demand periods while ensuring that the customer acceptance rate remains relatively stable. A high demand period (like Day 3) justifies a price increase, even if it results in a slight decrease in customer acceptance.

- **Revenue Maximization**: On higher-demand days, the RL agent is able to boost prices and maximize revenue. The revenue increase on

Day 3 (from $5500 on Day 1 to $9000 on Day 3) indicates that the RL model effectively capitalizes on opportunities when demand is strong.

- **Balance Between Acceptance and Efficiency**: Although higher prices might lead to lower customer acceptance, the company is still able to achieve a good balance between maintaining operational efficiency and achieving higher revenues.

Supply Chain Management Decisions:

- **Flexible Pricing Strategy**: The logistics company should consider implementing a more flexible pricing strategy that adjusts dynamically in response to fluctuations in demand. This could be a competitive advantage, especially for last-mile delivery, where prices are highly sensitive to time and service quality.

- **Customer Behavior Analysis**: Further analysis could be done to understand customer segments better. For example, if certain customer segments (e.g., urgent deliveries) are less sensitive to price changes, the company could apply targeted price adjustments for different customer groups.

- **Operational Efficiency**: Since delivery efficiency remains consistently high, the company should continue investing in process improvements that optimize delivery routes, staff utilization, and vehicle deployment, ensuring that any price increase does not negatively impact service quality.

- **Real-time Pricing Adjustments**: The RL model could be implemented in real-time systems, allowing for dynamic price changes throughout the day based on customer behavior, competitor pricing, and market conditions.

8. Real-Time Analytics and IoT in Supply Chains

Real-time analytics and the Internet of Things (IoT) are revolutionizing the way supply chains operate. By connecting devices, sensors, and software to collect and analyze data instantaneously, businesses can gain unprecedented visibility into their supply chain operations. This technology allows companies to monitor inventory levels, track shipments, and detect issues in real-time, rather than relying on outdated data or waiting for periodic reports. As a result, businesses can respond more quickly to changes, disruptions, or inefficiencies in the supply chain.

IoT devices such as RFID tags, GPS trackers, and sensors are embedded in products, containers, or equipment, sending data about their location, temperature, and condition to a central system. This constant stream of data gives companies a clearer picture of their operations and helps them identify potential problems before they escalate. For example, if a shipment is delayed, or a piece of equipment is malfunctioning, the system can instantly alert the relevant parties, allowing for faster intervention and mitigation.

With real-time analytics, organizations can also forecast demand more accurately. By analyzing historical data and incorporating real-time information, businesses can predict trends, optimize stock levels, and avoid overstocking or understocking products. This leads to better resource allocation, more efficient use of warehouse space, and reduced operational costs. It also minimizes the risk of stockouts, which can lead to lost sales, or excess inventory, which can tie up capital and incur storage fees.

Real-time analytics also enables smarter decision-making. With the ability to access live data, decision-makers can identify emerging trends, assess supplier performance, and make adjustments on the fly. For instance, if a supplier is consistently late with deliveries, businesses can quickly switch to a more reliable one, reducing disruptions and maintaining supply chain continuity. Additionally, the data can be used to optimize delivery routes, improving efficiency and cutting transportation costs.

Incorporating real-time analytics into supply chains also improves customer satisfaction. When companies can track shipments in real time and provide customers with accurate delivery updates, it builds trust and reliability. Moreover, IoT sensors can help ensure that products are kept within the required conditions, such as temperature-controlled items, reducing the risk of damage and ensuring quality. Customers are more likely to remain loyal when they receive their products on time and in perfect condition.

Overall, the integration of IoT and real-time analytics in supply chains enhances transparency, efficiency, and responsiveness. As businesses increasingly adopt these technologies, they gain a competitive edge by improving operational performance, reducing costs, and delivering superior customer service. The combination of connected devices and instant data analysis is transforming the supply chain landscape, creating a more agile, data-driven environment that can adapt to the complexities of today's fast-paced global markets.

Practical Example Context: Real-Time Analytics and IoT in Supply Chains

A global supply chain management company is leveraging real-time analytics and Internet of Things (IoT) technology to monitor and manage its warehouse inventory, transportation systems, and product flow. IoT sensors are placed on various assets, such as delivery trucks and storage units, providing real-time data on stock levels, shipment conditions, and location. The data is collected and analyzed using real-time analytics to make timely decisions on inventory replenishment, optimize delivery routes, and identify potential disruptions like delays or spoilage. For instance, the company monitors temperature-sensitive products like pharmaceuticals, ensuring they remain within the required temperature range during transit.

Sample Data

Asset	Location	Stock Level	Temperature (°C)	Delivery Status	Estimated Time of Arrival (ETA)
Truck #1	Warehouse A	500 units	5°C	In Transit	3 hours
Truck #2	Warehouse B	1000 units	10°C	In Transit	2.5 hours
Truck #3	Warehouse C	300 units	7°C	Delayed	4 hours
Warehouse D	Location D	800 units	N/A	Stock Available	N/A

- Load the Data into a data analysis software / tool

- Analyze the data.

Output and Results

1. **Truck #1**: The stock level is sufficient (500 units), and the temperature is within the acceptable range (5°C). The truck is on time with an ETA of 3 hours.

2. **Truck #2**: The stock level is high (1000 units) and the temperature is acceptable (10°C). The truck will arrive in 2.5 hours, indicating that replenishment needs are well-handled.

3. **Truck #3**: There is a smaller stock level (300 units) and a slight temperature deviation (7°C), but the truck is delayed by an additional 30 minutes, which may require investigation to ensure no negative impact on the product.

4. **Warehouse D**: Stock level is stable (800 units) but no temperature data is available for this location, which is a potential gap in monitoring.

Interpretation of Results

- **Stock Level Management**: Stock levels are being monitored effectively across different locations. However, Truck #3's stock level is low, which could mean the supply is running low and may need replenishment soon.

- **Temperature Sensitivity**: Trucks #1 and #2 show acceptable temperature levels, which is critical for sensitive goods. Truck #3, with a slightly elevated temperature (7°C), could face risks, especially if the temperature-sensitive products are pharmaceuticals.

- **Delays and Impact**: The delay of Truck #3 might be due to traffic or other logistical issues. The real-time alert system allows for proactive intervention, potentially rerouting or informing the warehouse to adjust customer expectations.

- **Data Gaps**: Warehouse D lacks temperature data, which poses a risk in monitoring perishable or sensitive goods.

Observations

- **Efficiency**: The real-time monitoring system is enhancing operational efficiency by providing live data on delivery status, stock levels, and conditions.

- **Vulnerability**: There is a gap in temperature monitoring at Warehouse D. While stock levels are adequate, temperature sensitivity could be overlooked in future deliveries.

- **Delay Management**: The delayed delivery of Truck #3 needs closer inspection. In real-time analytics, delay patterns could lead to adjustments in scheduling or even inventory reallocation to ensure customer satisfaction.

Decisions from the Supply Chain Management Perspective

1. **Inventory Replenishment**: Truck #3 should be prioritized for restocking or rerouting to avoid stockouts. Proactively monitoring low stock levels will help optimize inventory flows.

2. **Temperature Monitoring**: Temperature sensors should be installed at Warehouse D to close the gap in the data collection. If temperature-sensitive products are handled here, immediate action is necessary to ensure compliance with storage conditions.

3. **Delay Mitigation**: Proactively monitor delays. For Truck #3, the delay should trigger an alert to both warehouse staff and customers for rescheduling deliveries or offering alternative routes. This decision ensures minimal disruption in customer service.

4. **Route Optimization**: Real-time analytics and IoT data can further optimize transportation routes for Trucks #1 and #2, particularly by identifying factors such as traffic or weather conditions, reducing delivery times and costs.

This real-time decision-making process strengthens the overall efficiency and resilience of the supply chain, ensuring that the company can respond to potential issues swiftly.

8.1 Role of IoT in Data Collection

The Internet of Things (IoT) has significantly changed how data is collected in various industries. By connecting everyday objects to the internet, IoT devices enable the gathering of real-time data from sources that were previously difficult or even impossible to monitor. These devices include everything from wearable fitness trackers to industrial machines, smart home devices, and even agricultural sensors. This constant flow of data provides businesses, researchers, and governments with the ability to monitor systems, processes, and environments continuously, helping them make informed decisions.

In industries like healthcare, IoT devices can track patient vitals, medication adherence, and activity levels, sending this information to healthcare professionals for continuous monitoring. This real-time data allows for early intervention in case of any abnormalities, improving patient outcomes. Similarly, in manufacturing, IoT sensors can monitor equipment performance, detecting issues like malfunctions or wear and tear before they lead to expensive breakdowns. This predictive maintenance approach not only reduces downtime but also extends the lifespan of machinery.

IoT's role in environmental monitoring is another crucial example of how data collection has been revolutionized. Devices can now monitor air and water quality, track pollution levels, and even detect hazardous weather conditions. This data helps governments and organizations take timely actions to address environmental risks, ultimately leading to better sustainability practices. It also allows researchers to study climate change and other environmental issues with far more accuracy, as they can rely on constant, real-time data from across the globe.

In agriculture, IoT devices are making a significant impact by helping farmers collect data on soil moisture, weather patterns, and crop health. This data can be used to optimize irrigation, reduce water waste, and improve crop yields. Sensors in the soil and on farm equipment provide farmers with detailed insights that help them make better decisions about planting, fertilizing, and harvesting, ultimately increasing productivity and profitability while reducing environmental impact.

IoT also plays a role in improving consumer experiences through smart devices. Smart homes, for instance, collect data about how individuals interact with their living environments. Thermostats, lighting systems, and security cameras gather data that can be analyzed to create more personalized experiences for homeowners. By using this information, devices can learn preferences, adjust settings automatically, and even predict future needs, enhancing convenience and energy efficiency.

The vast amount of data collected through IoT devices also presents significant challenges related to privacy, security, and data management. As more devices are connected and data is continuously generated, ensuring the security of this information becomes a top priority. Companies must implement robust systems to store, analyze, and protect the data they collect, while also being transparent about how they use it. Despite these challenges, IoT's potential in transforming data collection is immense, providing insights that were once unimaginable.

Practical Example: Tracking Inventory in Real-Time Using IoT Sensors in a Warehouse

In a large e-commerce warehouse, IoT sensors are installed on shelves and bins to track the real-time movement and stock levels of inventory. These sensors relay data to a centralized management system that allows warehouse managers to monitor stock levels, detect product movement, and trigger automatic replenishment when needed. The system is integrated with the warehouse's ERP (Enterprise Resource Planning) to ensure seamless data flow between inventory management, order fulfillment, and procurement teams.

Sample Data in Table

Product ID	Product Name	Initial Stock	Current Stock	Restock Threshold	Stock Movement	Timestamp
P001	Wireless Mouse	500	450	100	Sold 50	2025-01-14 09:00:00
P002	USB Keyboard	300	280	50	Sold 20	2025-01-14 09:00:00
P003	Laptop Charger	150	130	30	Sold 20	2025-01-14 09:00:00
P004	Bluetooth Speaker	100	90	20	Sold 10	2025-01-14 09:00:00
P005	Webcam	200	190	40	Sold 10	2025-01-14 09:00:00

- Load the Data into a data analysis software / tool

- Analyze the data.

Output and Results

- **Restock Threshold**: Each product has a defined minimum threshold below which stock levels should be replenished. For example, the Wireless Mouse (P001) has a threshold of 100 units.

- **Stock Movement**: This column tracks the number of units sold since the last data update.

- **Real-Time Stock Level**: Real-time stock levels are updated based on sales data. For instance, after selling 50 units, the Wireless Mouse's stock level is reduced from 500 to 450 units.

Interpretation and Results

1. **Wireless Mouse (P001)**: The stock level is now 450 units, which is above the restock threshold of 100. No immediate replenishment is required at this point.

2. **USB Keyboard (P002)**: The stock level is 280, above the restock threshold of 50, but it's important to monitor closely as it is relatively close to the threshold.

3. **Laptop Charger (P003)**: The stock is at 130, above the threshold of 30. Given the sales rate, it is likely that this product will need to be replenished soon, especially if the movement continues at the same pace.

4. **Bluetooth Speaker (P004)**: With a stock of 90 units, this product is near its restock threshold of 20, indicating that it may need to be reordered soon to avoid stockouts.

5. **Webcam (P005)**: The current stock of 190 units is well above the threshold of 40. No immediate action is needed for replenishment.

Observations

- **High Sales Velocity**: Products like the Wireless Mouse and Laptop Charger show significant sales, with movement of 50 and 20 units, respectively, in the given time period. This suggests that these products are in high demand and should be prioritized for replenishment when stock gets closer to thresholds.

- **Approaching Replenishment Thresholds**: The Bluetooth Speaker (P004) is close to its restock threshold, indicating it may face a stockout risk if sales continue at the same rate.

- **Effective Stock Management**: The real-time tracking allows warehouse managers to detect stock movement patterns and anticipate demand, leading to more accurate and proactive decision-making for reordering.

Decisions from a Supply Chain Management Perspective

1. **Proactive Replenishment**: Based on the real-time stock data, the warehouse management system could trigger automated reorder alerts for products nearing their restock thresholds, ensuring that orders are placed before stockouts occur.

2. **Demand Forecasting**: The system can provide insights into sales velocity, allowing the supply chain team to forecast demand more accurately. For example, the Wireless Mouse's rapid sales could indicate an upcoming surge in demand, so the procurement team might place larger orders with suppliers.

3. **Optimizing Stock Levels**: The observation that the Bluetooth Speaker is nearing its threshold, even though other products have ample stock, suggests that product-specific demand patterns are being tracked and monitored. This allows the warehouse to allocate space and resources more efficiently.

4. **Inventory Audits**: Real-time inventory tracking ensures that discrepancies between physical and digital stock levels are minimized. Regular audits become more efficient when combined with IoT technology, reducing human error and ensuring accurate stock data at all times.

In conclusion, using IoT sensors for real-time inventory tracking enables warehouse managers and supply chain professionals to make informed, data-driven decisions. This leads to better stock management, improved customer satisfaction through timely fulfillment, and optimized resource utilization.

8.2 Real-Time Supply Chain Visibility

Real-time supply chain visibility refers to the ability of organizations to monitor and track their supply chain operations as they happen. This means companies can observe the movement of goods, inventory levels, and other critical data instantaneously. With this capability, businesses can better understand what's happening within their supply chains at any given moment, from raw material suppliers to end customers. This visibility enables proactive management and decision-making, ensuring that issues are identified and addressed quickly before they cause significant disruptions.

The integration of advanced technologies, such as sensors, GPS tracking, and cloud-based platforms, has played a significant role in making real-time visibility possible. These technologies collect and transmit data continuously, providing companies with up-to-the-minute insights. For example, using GPS on delivery trucks allows organizations to track shipments in transit, offering real-time location updates. Similarly, sensors within warehouses or on products help monitor inventory levels and environmental conditions, ensuring goods are stored appropriately.

A key benefit of real-time visibility is improved decision-making. When companies have up-to-the-minute information about supply chain activities, they can make more informed decisions. For instance, if a shipment is delayed, businesses can quickly reroute or reschedule deliveries to minimize the impact. This ability to act fast helps mitigate risks and reduces the likelihood of operational bottlenecks, ultimately leading to more efficient supply chain operations.

Moreover, real-time visibility enhances collaboration across the entire supply chain. Different stakeholders, from suppliers to customers, can access the same data, fostering transparency and trust. By sharing information in real time, partners can synchronize their efforts, align expectations, and respond faster to challenges. This increased collaboration can improve overall supply chain performance and customer satisfaction.

Another significant advantage is the potential for cost savings. With real-time visibility, businesses can identify inefficiencies or waste within their supply chains, such as overstocking or transportation delays. Addressing these issues promptly helps reduce costs associated with inventory management, transportation, and warehousing. Moreover, by optimizing routes and improving stock levels, companies can streamline operations and cut down on unnecessary expenses.

Lastly, real-time supply chain visibility supports greater resilience in the face of disruptions. Whether it's a natural disaster, labor strike, or sudden demand spike, organizations can respond quickly to changing conditions. By monitoring the flow of goods and information, businesses can adapt to unforeseen circumstances with greater agility. This level of preparedness strengthens the supply chain's ability to continue operating smoothly, even during challenging times.

Practical Example: Improving Supply Chain Visibility with IoT Devices for Temperature-Sensitive Products

A pharmaceutical company transports temperature-sensitive vaccines across various distribution points to healthcare facilities. To ensure the vaccines remain within the required temperature range (2°C to 8°C), IoT-enabled temperature sensors are attached to each shipment. These sensors transmit real-time temperature data to a centralized platform, allowing the company to monitor conditions continuously throughout the journey. The company uses this data to track and respond to any deviations from the desired temperature range, ensuring product integrity and compliance with health regulations.

Sample Data (Before and After IoT Implementation):

Shipment ID	Start Temp (°C)	End Temp (°C)	Avg Temp (°C)	Max Temp (°C)	Min Temp (°C)	Delivery Time (hrs)	Temperature Deviation (hrs)
001	4.0	7.5	5.5	8.2	3.8	12	0
002	3.8	9.0	6.4	10.0	3.0	10	1
003	5.5	8.2	6.8	9.0	4.5	14	2
004	2.0	5.5	4.0	7.5	1.5	16	0
005	4.2	8.5	6.0	9.5	3.2	11	1

- Load the Data into a data analysis software / tool
- Analyze the data.

Output and Results Interpretation:

- **Temperature Deviations**: The table shows the temperature deviations for each shipment, measured in hours. For example,

Shipment 002 experienced a deviation of 1 hour, with the temperature rising above the 8°C threshold at some point during transit.

- **Avg Temp and Max Temp**: For Shipment 003, the average temperature was 6.8°C, and the maximum temperature reached 9.0°C. While still within range, this fluctuation indicates the importance of real-time monitoring to identify and mitigate risks.

- **Delivery Time**: The shipment durations vary, with the longest delivery time being 16 hours (Shipment 004). Longer durations increase the risk of potential temperature issues.

Observations:

1. **Temperature Fluctuations**: Even within the acceptable range (2°C - 8°C), some shipments experienced minor temperature spikes (e.g., Shipment 003). Continuous monitoring allows for early intervention if these fluctuations exceed thresholds.

2. **Impact of Shipping Duration**: Longer transit times (e.g., Shipment 004 with 16 hours) provide more opportunities for temperature deviations to occur, increasing the need for more robust monitoring solutions.

3. **Temperature Compliance**: In all cases, the average temperatures remained close to the target range, but real-time data indicated moments where the temperature was approaching the upper limit. Without this visibility, these risks might have gone unnoticed.

Supply Chain Management Decisions:

1. **Enhanced Monitoring**: Based on the observed fluctuations, the company should consider deploying additional IoT sensors with more frequent data transmission intervals, or augment the shipment with better temperature-controlled packaging solutions.

2. **Routing Optimization**: Longer delivery times contributed to more significant temperature fluctuations. The company should evaluate faster, more efficient shipping routes, even if they come at a higher cost.

3. **Real-time Alerts and Response**: Implement a system for automated alerts whenever a temperature breach is detected, triggering corrective actions like rerouting or accelerating delivery.

4. **Collaborate with Logistics Providers**: Ensure that logistics partners are equipped with similar IoT solutions for full visibility across the entire supply chain, allowing for quicker interventions if issues arise.

By implementing IoT devices, the company gains invaluable insight into its supply chain's real-time conditions, which helps minimize risks to product quality and regulatory compliance. The data empowers decision-makers to take proactive steps and enhance overall supply chain efficiency.

8.3 Analytics for Real-Time Decision Making

In today's fast-paced world, the ability to make real-time decisions is crucial for businesses and organizations across various sectors. Real-time decision-making relies on the ability to collect, process, and analyze data as it becomes available. This allows decision-makers to respond swiftly to emerging situations, opportunities, or challenges. The more accurate and timely the data, the better the decisions that can be made, ensuring that businesses stay competitive and agile in a constantly changing environment.

One of the main drivers of real-time decision-making is the rapid advancement of technology. With the rise of big data, cloud computing, and the Internet of Things (IoT), organizations now have access to vast amounts of information in real time. This allows them to track customer behavior, monitor market trends, and assess operational performance instantaneously. The availability of this data provides a clear advantage, enabling businesses to not only respond quickly to current circumstances but also to predict potential issues before they arise.

Real-time analytics offers a distinct edge in various industries, including retail, healthcare, finance, and logistics. In retail, for example, businesses can use real-time data to adjust pricing, optimize inventory, and personalize customer experiences on the fly. In healthcare, real-time analytics can assist doctors in diagnosing conditions, monitoring patients, and adjusting treatment plans as necessary. Similarly, in finance, firms can analyze market movements and adjust trading strategies in near real-time, minimizing risk and maximizing opportunities.

A critical component of real-time decision-making is the ability to synthesize and interpret complex data sets. It is not enough to simply collect data; it must be processed and analyzed in a way that is meaningful and actionable. This requires the use of advanced analytics tools, artificial intelligence, and machine learning algorithms that can extract insights from raw data and present them in a digestible format. The goal is to enable decision-makers to act on the information quickly, without getting bogged down in the complexities of data analysis.

Despite its advantages, real-time decision-making is not without its challenges. One of the main obstacles is ensuring data accuracy and reliability. Real-time data can sometimes be noisy or incomplete, which may lead to flawed conclusions if not handled carefully. Additionally, organizations need to invest in the right infrastructure to support real-time analytics, which can be resource-intensive. Ensuring data security is also critical, as the constant flow of data presents an increased risk of breaches or misuse.

Ultimately, real-time decision-making enhances an organization's ability to stay ahead of the curve and adapt to changing circumstances. By leveraging real-time analytics, businesses can make informed decisions that drive growth, improve efficiency, and reduce risk. As technology continues to evolve, the scope of real-time analytics will only expand, offering even more opportunities for businesses to improve their decision-making processes and outcomes.

Practical Example: Using Real-Time Data to Improve Fleet Routing and Scheduling Efficiency

In a logistics company that delivers goods to various retail stores, the fleet routing and scheduling system must adapt to real-time data, such as traffic conditions, weather, delivery windows, and vehicle status (e.g., fuel levels, vehicle breakdowns). The company is using GPS tracking, traffic monitoring, and weather data to optimize the routes and schedules for deliveries. Real-time adjustments are made to prevent delays and ensure on-time deliveries. Here's how the system works in practice.

Sample Data Table (Before Real-Time Adjustments)

Vehicle ID	Scheduled Route	Distance (km)	Estimated Time (hrs)	Traffic Status	Delivery Window (hrs)	Delay Factor (min)	Fuel Status (L)
V1	Route A	50	1.0	Moderate	9:00 AM - 11:00 AM	0	30
V2	Route B	70	1.5	Heavy	10:00 AM - 12:00 PM	30	25
V3	Route C	100	2.0	Light	12:00 PM - 2:00 PM	0	50

Vehicle ID	Scheduled Route	Distance (km)	Estimated Time (hrs)	Traffic Status	Delivery Window (hrs)	Delay Factor (min)	Fuel Status (L)
V4	Route D	40	0.8	Moderate	9:30 AM - 11:00 AM	10	35

- Load the Data into a data analysis software / tool
- Analyze the data.

Real-Time Data Adjustments (After Analysis)

After analyzing real-time traffic and weather data, as well as vehicle status, the system suggests the following changes:

1. **V1 (Route A)**: Traffic congestion near the route, adding 15 minutes of delay. The driver is rerouted to avoid this, reducing travel time by 10 minutes.
2. **V2 (Route B)**: Heavy traffic predicted to worsen, so the route is adjusted to a less congested alternative, reducing travel time by 20 minutes.
3. **V3 (Route C)**: Route remains unaffected, no changes made.
4. **V4 (Route D)**: A breakdown in the area of Route D leads to a 15-minute delay, so the driver is reassigned to another nearby route.

Results Table (After Adjustments)

Vehicle ID	Adjusted Route	Adjusted Distance (km)	Adjusted Time (hrs)	Adjusted Delivery Window	Adjusted Delay Factor (min)	Fuel Status (L)
V1	Route A	50	0.9	9:00 AM - 11:00 AM	0	30
V2	Route B	60	1.2	10:00 AM - 12:00 PM	10	25
V3	Route C	100	2.0	12:00 PM - 2:00 PM	0	50

Vehicle ID	Adjusted Route	Adjusted Distance (km)	Adjusted Time (hrs)	Adjusted Delivery Window	Adjusted Delay Factor (min)	Fuel Status (L)
V4	Route E	45	0.9	9:30 AM - 11:00 AM	10	35

Interpretation and Observations:

1. **V1 (Route A)**: The real-time data allowed the system to optimize the route, reducing the travel time by 10 minutes. This resulted in no delay and still meets the delivery window.

2. **V2 (Route B)**: By rerouting due to heavy traffic, the vehicle's total distance traveled decreased by 10 km, and travel time was reduced by 20 minutes, which helps meet the delivery deadline.

3. **V3 (Route C)**: Since no real-time traffic or weather issues affected the route, no adjustments were made. The vehicle continues with the planned route.

4. **V4 (Route D)**: A vehicle breakdown led to a re-route, but the delivery was still on time due to efficient reassignment to Route E, resulting in a slight distance and time adjustment.

Decisions from Supply Chain Management Perspective:

- **Proactive Routing and Scheduling**: Leveraging real-time data allows the company to make proactive decisions. Rerouting vehicles based on traffic and weather can reduce delays and optimize fleet utilization.

- **Resource Utilization**: By monitoring vehicle statuses (e.g., fuel levels, breakdowns), resources can be more effectively allocated, reducing downtime and improving fleet efficiency.

- **Customer Satisfaction**: Real-time adjustments lead to better on-time deliveries, which enhances customer satisfaction and retention.

- **Cost Savings**: By reducing fuel consumption through optimized routes and improving delivery times, the company can save on operational costs, including fuel and labor.

In conclusion, using real-time data enhances the ability to adjust to changing circumstances, improving overall fleet efficiency and reducing the likelihood of delays. Supply Chain Managers should prioritize technologies that provide real-time data and integration capabilities to optimize their routing and scheduling strategies continuously.

9. Risk Management and Resilience with Data Science

Risk management is about identifying, assessing, and prioritizing risks to minimize their impact on an organization. It is a crucial process for businesses to ensure that they are prepared for potential challenges. In the past, this often relied on manual methods, such as surveys and historical data analysis, but with the rise of data science, organizations now have more powerful tools at their disposal. By leveraging advanced data analytics, businesses can gain deeper insights into risk patterns, enabling them to make more informed decisions about how to manage these risks.

Data science plays a significant role in this process by providing sophisticated models and algorithms to identify risks before they escalate. Machine learning, for example, can be used to predict potential risks based on historical data and current trends. It enables organizations to monitor risks in real time and take preventive measures before they become critical. By analyzing large datasets, data science can help uncover hidden risks that traditional methods may miss, offering a more comprehensive view of an organization's exposure to threats.

One of the key advantages of using data science in risk management is its ability to improve decision-making. Through predictive analytics, organizations can forecast potential outcomes and simulate various scenarios to understand the impact of different risk events. This helps leaders choose the best course of action, whether it involves mitigating, avoiding, or accepting the risk. With better data-driven insights, organizations can align their risk management strategies with their overall business objectives, ensuring that they are prepared for a wide range of possibilities.

Resilience, in the context of risk management, refers to an organization's ability to recover and adapt to disruptions. Data science supports resilience by helping organizations build more robust systems that can withstand and quickly recover from setbacks. By analyzing past incidents and understanding the factors that contributed to their impact, businesses can improve their systems and processes to reduce vulnerability. Moreover, predictive models can help businesses anticipate challenges, allowing them to develop strategies that enhance their ability to bounce back.

The integration of data science into resilience planning allows organizations to optimize their resources and maintain business continuity during a crisis. Real-time monitoring, combined with advanced analytics, enables companies to track disruptions and deploy resources effectively. For example, in industries such as finance or supply chain management, real-time data analysis can ensure that resources are diverted to critical areas when needed, helping minimize the disruption's impact. This proactive approach ensures that organizations are not just surviving crises but emerging stronger from them.

In conclusion, the combination of risk management and resilience through data science offers businesses a more agile and informed approach to handling uncertainties. Data science enhances the ability to predict and prepare for risks, while also supporting the resilience required to recover from disruptions. By embracing these tools, organizations can stay ahead of potential threats, navigate challenges with greater confidence, and ultimately achieve long-term sustainability. As technology continues to evolve, the role of data science in risk management and resilience will only become more critical to the success of businesses worldwide.

Practical Example: Risk Management and Resilience in Supply Chain with Data Science

In a supply chain scenario, a company wants to assess the resilience of its suppliers to potential disruptions, such as natural disasters, political instability, or demand fluctuations. Using data science, the company conducts a risk analysis by evaluating key factors such as supplier lead times, financial stability, geographic location, and historical performance in the face of disruptions. The goal is to identify which suppliers are most vulnerable and which need more strategic interventions to improve resilience.

Sample Data:

Supplier	Lead Time (Days)	Financial Stability (1-10)	Location Risk (1-10)	Historical Disruption (1-10)	Resilience Score (1-10)
A	30	8	6	3	6
B	15	4	9	8	5
C	45	7	3	2	7
D	20	9	4	5	8
E	60	3	8	9	4

- Load the Data into a data analysis software / tool

- Analyze the data.

Risk Management and Resilience Calculation:

To assess the overall resilience, we can calculate a "Resilience Score" by aggregating the financial stability, location risk, and historical disruption metrics. The lower the risk, the higher the resilience. The lead time is factored separately as a potential delay risk but is normalized into the final resilience score. A weighted average formula could be used for this, where each factor contributes equally.

For simplicity, let's assume the formula for calculating the Resilience Score is:

Resilience Score

$$= \left(\frac{\text{Financial Stability} + (10 - \text{Location Risk}) + (10 - \text{Historical Disruption})}{3} \right)$$

Output and Results:

Supplier	Lead Time (Days)	Financial Stability (1-10)	Location Risk (1-10)	Historical Disruption (1-10)	Resilience Score (1-10)
A	30	8	6	3	6
B	15	4	9	8	3.67
C	45	7	3	2	7.33
D	20	9	4	5	8
E	60	3	8	9	2.33

Interpretation of Results:

- **Supplier D** has the highest resilience score (8), which indicates that, despite having moderate lead times, it has strong financial stability, low location risk, and a relatively better historical performance during disruptions.

- **Supplier C** also performs well (Resilience Score of 7.33), mainly because of its lower location and disruption risks, even though its lead time is longer.

- **Supplier A** shows moderate resilience (6) with balanced risk factors, but it still faces vulnerabilities in comparison to others.

- **Supplier B** has the lowest resilience score (3.67), reflecting its weak financial stability, high location risk, and a poor historical track record during disruptions.

- **Supplier E** is the least resilient (2.33), primarily due to its high location and disruption risks, coupled with a very low financial stability score.

Observations:

- Lead time does not directly correlate to resilience, but it may indirectly indicate the potential impact of disruptions. For example, Supplier E has the longest lead time (60 days), yet its resilience score is still low due to other factors.

- Financial stability and historical disruption performance appear to have the strongest impact on resilience. Suppliers B and E are particularly vulnerable due to poor financial health and frequent historical disruptions.

- Supplier D is the most resilient despite having an average lead time, due to its overall stability.

Decisions from the Supply Chain Management Perspective:

- **Supplier Diversification**: The company should consider diversifying its suppliers, especially replacing Supplier B and Supplier E, as their low resilience could lead to significant disruptions. It may also be beneficial to have alternative suppliers ready for these high-risk suppliers.

- **Risk Mitigation Plans**: For Supplier A, which has a moderate score, a more detailed risk mitigation plan should be developed to prepare for any future disruptions. They might be a good candidate for increased inventory buffers or closer monitoring of financial health.

- **Resilience Investment**: For Supplier D and Supplier C, the company should focus on strengthening their relationships and consider increasing the order volume from these suppliers, given their high resilience. These suppliers could be valuable for long-term stability.

- **Lead Time Management**: Suppliers with high lead times (like Supplier E) should be evaluated further for potential risks, and the company may want to establish faster alternative routes or backup suppliers for urgent orders.

This analysis helps the company identify where to focus resources, whether through improving supplier relationships, investing in risk mitigation, or diversifying to reduce supply chain vulnerability.

9.1 Identifying and Assessing Supply Chain Risks

Supply chain risks are potential disruptions or challenges that can affect the flow of goods, services, or information across the various stages of production and delivery. These risks can arise from a variety of factors, including natural disasters, geopolitical events, labor strikes, or supplier failures. The complexity of modern supply chains, which often span multiple countries and involve various stakeholders, can make it difficult to anticipate and address these risks effectively. A small disruption in one part of the supply chain can have a cascading effect on the entire system, impacting operations, costs, and customer satisfaction.

Identifying supply chain risks begins with understanding the various components of the supply chain and the dependencies between them. This involves mapping out the entire supply chain, from raw materials to final delivery, and identifying potential points of failure. Suppliers, transportation routes, and inventory management are all critical areas where risks can emerge. For example, a company that relies on a single supplier for a key component may face significant disruptions if that supplier faces production delays or quality issues. Similarly, transportation risks can arise from weather disruptions or political instability in transit regions.

Once risks have been identified, it's important to assess their potential impact on the supply chain. This includes considering the likelihood of each risk occurring and the severity of its impact if it does. Companies need to evaluate how risks might affect various aspects of their operations, such as production timelines, costs, and customer satisfaction. For example, if a supplier goes out of business, it could lead to delays and increased costs for alternative sourcing. Similarly, if transportation routes are disrupted, it could lead to inventory shortages or increased lead times.

To effectively assess supply chain risks, companies often conduct risk assessments, which can involve qualitative and quantitative analyses. Qualitative assessments may rely on expert judgment and scenario planning, while quantitative assessments can use historical data and statistical models to estimate the likelihood and impact of different risks. This process helps companies prioritize risks and determine which ones require immediate attention. For example, a risk that is highly likely to occur but has a relatively low impact may warrant less attention than a risk that is unlikely to occur but could cause significant damage.

Mitigation strategies for supply chain risks are essential for reducing their potential impact. One common approach is diversification, which involves sourcing materials or components from multiple suppliers or regions to reduce dependence on a single source. Another strategy is creating contingency plans, such as having backup suppliers or alternative transportation routes in place. Businesses can also invest in technology to improve supply chain visibility, such as tracking systems that monitor shipments in real-time. These technologies can help companies identify and address disruptions more quickly, minimizing their impact.

Finally, continuous monitoring and review of supply chain risks is crucial for ensuring long-term resilience. Supply chains are dynamic, and risks can change over time due to shifts in the market, regulations, or global events. By regularly assessing the risk landscape and adjusting mitigation strategies, companies can adapt to emerging threats and maintain a resilient and responsive supply chain. This proactive approach enables businesses to not only avoid disruptions but also to recover more swiftly when problems do arise, ultimately ensuring more stable and efficient operations.

Practical Example: Quantifying Risks in Supplier Networks Using Historical Disruption Data

A global electronics manufacturer relies on a network of suppliers for key components. Historical data from the past 3 years is used to quantify risks associated with potential disruptions in the supply chain. The company collects disruption data based on factors like supplier delivery delays, production downtime, geopolitical events, natural disasters, and quality issues. The company wants to assess the likelihood and impact of these risks to improve resilience in its supply chain and make more informed decisions about sourcing and inventory management.

Sample Data (Historical Disruption Data)

Supplier	Year	Disruption Type	Frequency (Occurrences/Year)	Impact on Production (Days Lost)	Disruption Duration (Days)	Estimated Financial Loss ($)
Supplier A	2021	Delivery Delay	3	5	2	10,000
Supplier A	2022	Quality Issue	1	7	4	25,000
Supplier B	2021	Geopolitical Event	2	10	5	50,000

Supplier	Year	Disruption Type	Frequency (Occurrences/Year)	Impact on Production (Days Lost)	Disruption Duration (Days)	Estimated Financial Loss ($)
Supplier B	2022	Natural Disaster	1	15	7	100,000
Supplier C	2021	Delivery Delay	4	3	3	12,000
Supplier C	2022	Production Downtime	1	12	6	60,000
Supplier D	2021	Quality Issue	2	6	4	30,000
Supplier D	2022	Delivery Delay	2	4	2	20,000

- Load the Data into a data analysis software / tool

- Analyze the data.

Output and Results

1. **Risk Frequency**: The frequency of disruptions per supplier is averaged across the years.

2. **Impact on Production**: The average number of days lost due to disruptions is calculated per supplier.

3. **Total Financial Loss**: The total estimated financial loss is derived from the total impact over the years.

Summary Table: Risk Quantification

Supplier	Avg. Frequency (per Year)	Avg. Impact on Production (Days Lost)	Avg. Disruption Duration (Days)	Total Estimated Financial Loss ($)
Supplier A	2	6	3	35,000

Supplier	Avg. Frequency (per Year)	Avg. Impact on Production (Days Lost)	Avg. Disruption Duration (Days)	Total Estimated Financial Loss ($)
Supplier B	1.5	12.5	6	150,000
Supplier C	2.5	5.5	3	72,000
Supplier D	2	5	3	50,000

Explanation and Interpretation of Results

- **Supplier A**: This supplier has a moderate frequency of disruptions (2 disruptions per year), but their impact on production is relatively low (6 days lost). The total financial loss is moderate ($35,000). This suggests that Supplier A is a relatively stable supplier, but some improvements in their logistics or quality control could help reduce risks.

- **Supplier B**: Despite the lower frequency of disruptions (1.5 per year), the impact on production is much higher (12.5 days lost). This supplier's disruptions, especially geopolitical events and natural disasters, are very costly ($150,000). Supplier B presents a high-risk profile and may require alternate sourcing strategies or additional insurance to mitigate the potential impact.

- **Supplier C**: Supplier C has the highest frequency of disruptions (2.5 per year), but the overall impact is moderate (5.5 days lost). Their financial loss is also moderate ($72,000). This suggests that while disruptions occur frequently, they may be relatively short-lived or manageable. Some investment in improving their reliability could reduce these risks.

- **Supplier D**: Supplier D has a moderate disruption frequency (2 per year) with low impact on production (5 days lost). Their financial loss is also moderate ($50,000). Supplier D is relatively stable, but improving their supply chain operations could further reduce the risk.

Observations

- **High-Risk Suppliers**: Supplier B stands out as the highest risk, given the severe impact of disruptions, despite their lower frequency. The company should consider diversifying its sourcing from this supplier or investing in risk mitigation strategies such as better forecasting, longer lead times, or even finding alternative suppliers.

- **Frequent but Lower-Impact Suppliers**: Suppliers like A and C have a higher frequency of disruptions but the financial and operational impact is relatively lower. The company may benefit from focusing on enhancing communication and process efficiencies with these suppliers to reduce the likelihood of these frequent disruptions.

- **Stable Suppliers**: Supplier D, while moderate in terms of disruptions and losses, may not require as much attention, but a proactive approach to keeping their performance stable will reduce potential future risks.

Supply Chain Management Decisions

1. **Diversification and Risk Mitigation**: For high-risk suppliers like Supplier B, the company should consider dual sourcing or implementing stronger contingency plans, such as safety stock or longer lead times, to mitigate the impact of geopolitical or natural disruptions.

2. **Supplier Collaboration**: For suppliers with frequent but less impactful disruptions (like Supplier A and C), the company can work on strengthening the relationship through collaborative problem-solving and setting up better contingency measures, reducing disruption frequency and duration.

3. **Improvement Focus**: For moderate-risk suppliers like Supplier D, continuous improvement programs could help reduce the financial losses caused by disruptions.

4. **Financial Planning**: In line with risk quantification, the company should account for these potential losses in its annual budgeting and risk management strategies to prepare for possible disruptions in future years.

By quantifying risks using historical disruption data, the company gains valuable insights into where to focus efforts to build a more resilient, efficient, and cost-effective supply chain.

9.2 Using Data Science for Risk Mitigation

Data science plays a crucial role in risk mitigation by enabling organizations to identify, assess, and manage potential threats in a proactive manner. By leveraging advanced analytics, organizations can detect patterns and trends within large datasets, allowing them to predict future risks with greater accuracy. For example, financial institutions use data science to identify suspicious transactions that may indicate fraudulent activity. By analyzing past transaction data, they can develop models that flag potentially fraudulent behavior, helping prevent significant financial losses.

One of the key methods in risk mitigation is predictive modeling, which uses historical data to forecast potential future risks. By training models on past events, businesses can gain insights into what types of risks are most likely to occur and when. This allows them to allocate resources more effectively, prioritizing the areas of highest risk. For example, in supply chain management, companies can predict disruptions due to factors like weather or political instability and adjust their plans accordingly.

Data science also helps in improving decision-making under uncertainty. With tools like machine learning and data visualization, companies can better understand complex scenarios and make informed decisions even when there is limited information. For instance, insurance companies use data science to assess the risk of insuring certain individuals or businesses by analyzing factors like claims history, geographical location, and other relevant data points. This allows them to set appropriate premiums and reduce the likelihood of major losses.

Another important aspect of data science in risk mitigation is anomaly detection. By continuously monitoring data streams in real-time, algorithms can identify unusual patterns that may signal emerging risks. In cybersecurity, for example, real-time monitoring of network traffic can detect unauthorized access or unusual activity, enabling a quick response to mitigate potential damage. This approach ensures that risks are addressed before they escalate into more significant problems.

Data science also enables companies to conduct scenario analysis, where various "what-if" scenarios are modeled to assess the impact of different risks. This technique allows businesses to evaluate how changes in variables, such as market conditions, regulatory changes, or technological advances, might affect their operations. By simulating different outcomes, companies can create contingency plans and be better prepared to adapt when faced with unexpected challenges.

Lastly, the integration of data science into risk management fosters a culture of continuous improvement. As more data is collected and analyzed, organizations can refine their risk models and improve their strategies over time. This feedback loop helps companies stay ahead of emerging risks and adapt to new threats in a dynamic environment. By using data-driven insights, businesses can ensure that they remain resilient and capable of mitigating risks more effectively.

Practical Example: Leveraging Predictive Analytics to Minimize Stockouts During High-Demand Seasons

A retail company anticipates high demand for its products during the holiday season, particularly for electronics. The company uses predictive analytics to forecast demand for specific products based on historical data, current market trends, and external factors such as promotions and weather patterns. The goal is to minimize stockouts and ensure product availability without overstocking, which can lead to excessive carrying costs. The company uses a demand forecasting model that incorporates machine learning algorithms to predict the demand for each product in the upcoming weeks of the high-demand season.

Sample Data: Predicted and Actual Demand for Electronics During Holiday Season

Week	Predicted Demand (Units)	Actual Demand (Units)	Stockouts (Units)	Overstock (Units)	Sales Revenue ($)	Supply Chain Cost ($)
1	1,200	1,150	50	0	115,000	5,000
2	1,500	1,600	100	0	160,000	6,500
3	1,300	1,200	0	100	120,000	5,200
4	1,800	1,750	50	0	175,000	7,000
5	1,600	1,550	50	0	155,000	6,000
6	1,700	1,750	100	0	175,000	6,500

- Load the Data into a data analysis software / tool
- Analyze the data.

Output and Results

- **Stockouts**: In Weeks 1, 2, 4, and 6, there were stockouts, indicating that the predictive model slightly underestimated demand in these weeks.

- **Overstock**: In Week 3, there was a small overstock (100 units), as actual demand was lower than predicted.

- **Sales Revenue**: Total sales revenue increased as actual demand matched closely with predicted demand, although stockouts slightly reduced potential sales.

- **Supply Chain Cost**: Supply chain costs fluctuated with the changes in demand. In weeks with stockouts, additional expedited shipping may have been required to meet customer needs, adding to the cost.

Interpretation of Results

1. **Accuracy of Predictions**: The predictive model's accuracy is quite high, but there are some discrepancies. Weeks 2, 4, and 6 faced stockouts, which suggests that the model may need refinement in predicting sudden spikes in demand, such as promotions or market shifts. Week 3 saw overstocking, indicating a potential opportunity to better predict lower-than-expected demand.

2. **Stockout Impact**: Stockouts lead to lost sales. For instance, in Week 2, 100 units were unavailable, and this resulted in a potential loss of $10,000 in revenue (100 units × $100 per unit). This should be factored into future forecasts to ensure better alignment with demand.

3. **Overstock Costs**: Overstock in Week 3 results in holding costs. If the 100 overstock units were not sold, it would lead to additional costs, such as storage and potential markdowns.

Observations

- **Overforecasting**: Some weeks (e.g., Week 3) experienced overforecasting, leading to a small overstock, which can contribute to higher costs. The model could benefit from including inventory buffers or considering market trends that might lead to lower-than-expected demand.

- **Underforecasting**: In high-demand weeks like Week 2, stockouts occurred because the model could not fully predict the surge in demand. This suggests the model should incorporate more real-time data (e.g., promotions or competitor actions) to adjust forecasts dynamically.

- **Supply Chain Responsiveness**: The supply chain was responsive but could be optimized further. For instance, faster replenishment strategies could have been employed in Week 2 to prevent stockouts without significantly increasing costs.

Supply Chain Management Decisions

- **Refining Forecasting Models**: Improve predictive models by incorporating external data like promotions, weather patterns, and competitor actions to better forecast demand spikes.

- **Inventory Buffering**: Introduce strategic safety stock levels based on historical demand variability, ensuring that even with inaccuracies in forecasts, stockouts are minimized.

- **Dynamic Replenishment**: Implement more dynamic replenishment strategies that adjust in real-time to changes in demand patterns, particularly during high-demand seasons.

- **Improve Supplier Relationships**: Work with suppliers to reduce lead times and increase the flexibility of deliveries during critical demand periods to ensure products are available when needed.

By leveraging predictive analytics, supply chain managers can enhance inventory planning, reduce the risk of stockouts, and improve overall profitability. The key is to continuously refine models with real-time data to ensure accurate demand forecasting in varying market conditions.

9.3 Building Resilient Supply Chains with Predictive Models

Supply chains are the backbone of global trade, but they are also vulnerable to various disruptions, such as natural disasters, geopolitical tensions, or sudden shifts in consumer demand. Building resilience within these supply chains has become crucial to ensuring businesses can adapt to unexpected challenges without significant losses. Predictive models are increasingly being recognized as a valuable tool in this effort, as they allow businesses to anticipate potential disruptions before they occur, enabling proactive rather than reactive decision-making.

These predictive models rely on vast amounts of historical data, including past disruptions, market trends, and other relevant variables. By analyzing this data, companies can identify patterns and correlations that may signal an impending issue. For example, a sudden spike in the price of raw materials or a disruption in transportation networks can be predicted by looking at similar events from the past. This foresight allows supply chain managers to adjust their strategies, such as securing alternative suppliers or increasing stock levels ahead of time, to mitigate the impact of these disruptions.

Another advantage of predictive models is their ability to simulate different scenarios and outcomes. By using advanced algorithms and machine learning techniques, these models can simulate how changes in one part of the supply chain might ripple through the entire network. This gives businesses a clearer understanding of the potential risks and enables them to plan more effectively. For example, if a supplier in a distant country is likely to face delays due to a natural disaster, the model might suggest adjusting inventory levels at various stages of production to compensate for this potential disruption.

In addition to forecasting disruptions, predictive models can also optimize the overall performance of the supply chain. They can help companies identify inefficiencies in their operations, such as excess inventory or underutilized transportation routes. By analyzing real-time data, these models can recommend improvements that reduce costs, shorten lead times, and increase flexibility. This optimization, when combined with predictive insights, ensures that a company's supply chain is both resilient and efficient.

Collaboration is also a critical element in building resilient supply chains, and predictive models facilitate better communication and coordination between suppliers, manufacturers, and distributors. By sharing insights generated by predictive analytics, each participant in the supply chain can make more informed decisions. This collective approach helps prevent disruptions from snowballing into larger, more costly problems. The more aligned the entire supply chain is, the better it can adapt to changes and recover from shocks.

Finally, building resilience through predictive models is not a one-time effort but an ongoing process. As market conditions evolve and new challenges emerge, these models need to be continually updated with fresh data to stay relevant. Companies must invest in technology and talent capable of refining these models and ensuring that they reflect the latest trends. With this commitment, businesses can create a supply chain that not only survives but thrives in an unpredictable world.

Practical Example Context: Designing a Risk-Resilient Logistics Network Using Machine Learning

In this scenario, a company is looking to design a logistics network that is resilient to various supply chain disruptions, including delays, weather events, and geopolitical risks. The company uses machine learning models to predict risks and optimize routing, inventory, and distribution strategies. The goal is to minimize the impact of disruptions on customer delivery times and costs while maximizing the reliability and efficiency of the supply chain.

Sample Data:

The machine learning model uses historical data on shipping times, supply chain interruptions, and weather-related disruptions. The model provides predictions on risk levels and suggests alternative routes or inventory management strategies.

Route	Historical Delivery Time (Days)	Predicted Disruption Risk (%)	Optimal Route Alternative	Predicted Cost Increase (%)	Expected Delivery Time After Optimization (Days)
A -> B	5	40	A -> C -> B	5	6

Route	Historical Delivery Time (Days)	Predicted Disruption Risk (%)	Optimal Route Alternative	Predicted Cost Increase (%)	Expected Delivery Time After Optimization (Days)
A -> C	4	30	No change	3	4
B -> D	6	60	B -> E -> D	8	7
C -> D	3	20	No change	2	3
D -> E	7	50	D -> F -> E	10	8

- Load the Data into a data analysis software / tool

- Analyze the data.

Output and Results Interpretation:

1. **Risk Prediction:**

   o The machine learning model predicts the disruption risk for each route, with the highest risk being observed for the route from **B -> D (60%)** and the lowest risk for **C -> D (20%)**.

   o The model suggests alternative routes to minimize risks. For instance, the **A -> B** route is predicted to face a 40% disruption risk, but an alternative via **A -> C -> B** increases the delivery time by 1 day and reduces risk significantly.

2. **Cost Impact:**

   o Routes with higher risks generally have higher cost increases due to the need for alternative routes or buffering inventory.

   o The route **B -> D** incurs the highest predicted cost increase of 8%, while **C -> D** sees only a 2% increase due to minimal risk.

3. **Optimized Delivery Time:**

- o Optimized delivery times vary by route. In high-risk scenarios (e.g., **A -> B**), the machine learning model suggests taking a longer route (**A -> C -> B**) to avoid disruptions, resulting in a slight increase in delivery time (from 5 to 6 days).

- o For lower-risk routes (**A -> C** and **C -> D**), no major changes in delivery times are needed.

Observations:

- The model suggests prioritizing routes with lower disruption risks, even if they slightly increase the delivery time or cost, to ensure consistent service delivery.

- Routes facing high disruption risks (like **B -> D**) should be modified to avoid potential delays, even if it results in slightly higher costs (like the increase of 8%).

- The **C -> D** route is stable, requiring no changes, as the risk is low and the cost increase is minimal.

Decisions from the Supply Chain Management Perspective:

1. **Optimization Prioritization:** The logistics network should prioritize routes with low risk and minimal cost increases, ensuring stable service levels. Routes with higher risk (e.g., **B -> D**) should be redesigned or avoided through rerouting.

2. **Cost Trade-Offs:** Decisions should balance between higher costs for risk mitigation and maintaining customer service levels. In cases of high-risk routes, accepting a slight cost increase may be necessary to maintain reliability.

3. **Continuous Monitoring:** Risk factors such as weather and geopolitical events should be continuously monitored, and machine learning models should be updated regularly to reflect changing conditions in the network.

4. **Inventory Buffers:** On high-risk routes, inventory buffers can be increased to mitigate potential delivery delays. For example, having a higher stock at distribution centers near high-risk routes can reduce the impact of delays on customer delivery times.

By integrating machine learning into logistics and supply chain management, companies can dynamically adjust their strategies to mitigate risks while balancing costs and service reliability.

10. Advanced Techniques for Supply Chain Optimization

Supply chain optimization is a continuous process that aims to improve efficiency, reduce costs, and enhance the overall performance of the supply chain. One of the key techniques involves demand forecasting, where advanced analytics and machine learning models are used to predict future customer demand based on historical data, seasonal trends, and external factors. These predictions allow companies to better align their production schedules and inventory levels with actual demand, reducing the risk of stockouts or excess inventory.

Another technique focuses on inventory management. By utilizing sophisticated inventory control systems, businesses can monitor stock levels in real time and implement just-in-time practices. This reduces the need for large warehouses, lowering storage costs and minimizing the risk of holding obsolete or excess products. Additionally, adopting multi-echelon inventory strategies allows companies to optimize the distribution of products across multiple locations, ensuring a smoother flow of goods throughout the entire supply chain.

Transportation optimization is also crucial for supply chain efficiency. Companies can leverage technologies like route optimization software to plan the most efficient delivery routes, reducing fuel costs and delivery times. Furthermore, the use of transportation management systems (TMS) enables businesses to better manage carrier relationships, optimize freight costs, and track shipments in real time. By consolidating shipments or using third-party logistics providers, companies can maximize their transportation capacity and further reduce operational expenses.

Supply chain visibility is an essential technique that involves the integration of various data sources across the supply chain. By using real-time tracking systems and collaborative platforms, companies gain full visibility into the movement of goods, inventory levels, and supplier performance. This transparency allows for quicker identification of potential disruptions, whether due to natural disasters, transportation delays, or supplier issues, enabling businesses to respond swiftly and maintain a steady flow of goods.

Risk management is another critical aspect of supply chain optimization. Companies must assess the potential risks at each stage of the supply chain, whether related to geopolitical events, financial instability, or natural hazards. By implementing contingency plans and diversifying suppliers, businesses can mitigate the impact of these risks. The use of predictive analytics and scenario modeling allows companies to foresee potential disruptions and take preemptive actions to minimize their effects on operations.

Finally, collaboration and communication with suppliers and other partners are fundamental to improving supply chain performance. By fostering strong relationships and information sharing, companies can align their goals with their suppliers, streamline procurement processes, and reduce lead times. Supplier performance management systems can help track and evaluate supplier reliability, allowing businesses to make more informed decisions about sourcing and building long-term partnerships that support mutual growth and efficiency.

Practical Example: Advanced Techniques for Supply Chain Optimization

A manufacturing company is facing challenges with its supply chain, particularly around inventory management, transportation, and supplier performance. The company decides to implement advanced optimization techniques using data analytics, machine learning, and simulation models to improve its supply chain performance. The company collects data on various parameters like demand forecasts, lead times, transportation costs, and supplier performance. They apply advanced techniques like **Predictive Analytics** for demand forecasting, **Genetic Algorithms** for optimizing transportation routes, and **Linear Programming** for inventory management. The goal is to minimize costs, improve delivery reliability, and ensure that inventory is optimized without overstocking or understocking.

Sample Data

Parameter	Value
Average Monthly Demand	50,000 units
Lead Time (Supplier)	10 days
Lead Time (Transport)	4 days
Cost per Unit (Supplier)	$20
Transportation Cost/Unit	$2
Inventory Carrying Cost	$0.5/unit/month

Parameter	Value
Safety Stock (Calculated)	8,000 units
Order Quantity (EOQ)	45,000 units

- Load the Data into a data analysis software / tool
- Analyze the data.

Output Results

Optimization Goal	Pre-Optimization	Post-Optimization
Total Transportation Cost ($)	50,000	45,000
Total Inventory Carrying Cost ($)	12,500	9,000
Total Supply Chain Cost ($)	95,000	85,000
On-time Delivery (%)	90%	98%
Overstock (%)	12%	5%
Stockouts (%)	8%	2%

Explanation and Interpretation of Results:

1. **Total Transportation Cost**: The optimization model helped reduce the total transportation cost by 10%. This was achieved by using **Genetic Algorithms** to optimize delivery routes and reduce inefficiencies in the supply chain.

2. **Inventory Carrying Cost**: Inventory carrying costs were reduced by optimizing the order quantities and reducing the **overstock** levels. With better demand forecasting and improved inventory policies, the company was able to minimize excess stock.

3. **Supply Chain Cost**: The total supply chain cost decreased by 10%, indicating that the applied optimization techniques successfully addressed multiple areas of inefficiency (transportation, inventory, and supplier management).

4. **On-time Delivery**: The on-time delivery rate increased from 90% to 98%. This improvement was a result of better demand forecasting

using **Predictive Analytics** and more reliable supplier performance modeling.

5. **Overstock and Stockouts**: Overstock levels dropped significantly, indicating improved inventory management. Stockouts were also minimized, suggesting that the company was able to maintain an appropriate level of safety stock and order quantities based on accurate demand forecasts.

Observations:

- By integrating **Predictive Analytics** and **Optimization Algorithms**, the company was able to reduce costs across key metrics while improving performance indicators like delivery reliability and inventory efficiency.

- The company was able to better match supply with demand, reducing waste (overstock) and ensuring customer demand was met (minimizing stockouts).

- The improvements in transportation cost and inventory carrying cost reflect the direct impact of optimizing routes and inventory policies based on accurate data.

Decisions from the Supply Chain Management Perspective:

- The company should continue to refine its demand forecasting models to ensure that the order quantities are as accurate as possible, minimizing both stockouts and overstock.

- Further investments in transportation optimization (e.g., advanced route planning or multi-modal transportation) could continue to reduce costs, especially with fluctuating fuel prices or supply chain disruptions.

- More collaboration with suppliers is essential to improve lead times and ensure reliability. Sharing demand forecasts and inventory data could help improve supplier performance and reduce variability.

- Ongoing monitoring of the system and its performance will be crucial to maintaining these improvements as market conditions change.

By applying these advanced techniques, the company has been able to achieve a balanced supply chain with reduced costs and improved service levels.

10.1 Genetic Algorithms and Simulated Annealing

Genetic Algorithms (GAs) are a class of optimization algorithms inspired by the process of natural evolution. They work by simulating the process of selection, crossover, and mutation, which are key principles in biological evolution. The algorithm starts with a population of potential solutions, often referred to as "individuals" or "chromosomes," which are encoded as strings, typically binary or real-valued numbers. Each individual is evaluated based on a fitness function, which determines how good the solution is relative to the problem being solved. Over time, individuals with higher fitness values are more likely to be selected for reproduction, mimicking the survival of the fittest concept in nature.

The reproduction process involves two main operators: crossover and mutation. Crossover combines two parent solutions to produce offspring, with the hope of creating better solutions by combining good features from both parents. Mutation introduces small, random changes to an individual's genes, allowing the population to explore new areas of the solution space and avoid local optima. These operations are applied iteratively over multiple generations, with the hope that the population gradually improves its overall fitness.

On the other hand, Simulated Annealing (SA) is an optimization technique inspired by the physical process of annealing, where a material is heated and then slowly cooled to reach a state of minimal energy. This process involves a random search of the solution space but uses a temperature parameter that controls the likelihood of accepting worse solutions as the algorithm progresses. Initially, when the temperature is high, the algorithm is more likely to accept worse solutions to escape local minima. As the temperature decreases, the algorithm becomes more conservative and is less likely to accept suboptimal solutions, eventually converging to a solution that approximates the global minimum.

Both Genetic Algorithms and Simulated Annealing are methods used to solve complex optimization problems, particularly those with large and poorly understood solution spaces. They are often applied in fields such as machine learning, operations research, and engineering design, where traditional optimization methods might fail to find solutions in a reasonable time. One key advantage of these techniques is their ability to explore vast, high-dimensional solution spaces without requiring a detailed understanding of the underlying problem structure.

Despite their similarities, GAs and SA differ in their approach to searching for solutions. GAs operate on a population of solutions and rely on iterative improvement through genetic operators, whereas SA works with a single solution at a time and uses temperature-based acceptance criteria to guide its search. The population-based nature of GAs allows for parallel exploration of multiple solutions, which can speed up the process of finding an optimal or near-optimal solution. In contrast, SA's single-solution focus can make it more susceptible to getting stuck in local minima, though it has the advantage of being simpler to implement and requiring fewer resources.

Both algorithms have their strengths and weaknesses, and the choice between them depends on the specific problem being addressed. GAs are generally more robust in complex, multimodal problems where there are many local optima, as their population-based approach helps prevent premature convergence. SA, however, can be more efficient in problems where the solution space is smooth and the global minimum can be reached with less exploration. In practice, hybrid approaches that combine the strengths of both algorithms are sometimes used to achieve better results in challenging optimization problems.

Practical Example: Using Genetic Algorithms for Optimizing Delivery Routes in a Multi-Vehicle Fleet

A logistics company is tasked with delivering goods to 6 different locations across a city using 3 delivery trucks. The company wants to minimize the total travel distance and time while ensuring that each truck serves a specific set of customers. Genetic algorithms (GAs) are employed to optimize the delivery routes by evolving populations of potential solutions through selection, crossover, and mutation processes. The problem is treated as a Traveling Salesman Problem (TSP) variant, where each truck must complete its route in the least possible distance without exceeding time or resource constraints.

Sample Data: The following table represents the distance (in kilometers) between each delivery location and the depot. The vehicles need to deliver to the locations marked from A to F.

Locations	Depot (D)	A	B	C	D	E	F
Depot (D)	0	10	15	20	25	30	35
A	10	0	5	10	15	20	25
B	15	5	0	7	12	17	22
C	20	10	7	0	5	10	15

Locations	Depot (D)	A	B	C	D	E	F
D	25	15	12	5	0	5	10
E	30	20	17	10	5	0	5
F	35	25	22	15	10	5	0

- Load the Data into a data analysis software / tool

- Analyze the data.

Genetic Algorithm Implementation

The genetic algorithm uses the following parameters:

- Population size: 10 individuals (possible routes)

- Crossover rate: 80%

- Mutation rate: 20%

- Generations: 100

Each individual (solution) represents a set of delivery routes for the three vehicles. Over generations, the algorithm selects the best solutions based on the fitness function, which is the total distance traveled.

Output and Results:

After running the genetic algorithm for 100 generations, the optimized routes for the three vehicles are:

Vehicle	Route	Distance (km)
Truck 1	D -> A -> B -> C	35
Truck 2	D -> E -> F -> D	45
Truck 3	D -> D -> D -> D	30

Explanation of Results:

- **Truck 1** is tasked with delivering to A, B, and C. The route minimizes travel distance between these locations, totaling 35 km.

- **Truck 2** handles locations E and F. The shortest route between these locations and the depot totals 45 km.

- **Truck 3** does not need to travel much because of constraints (perhaps a limited number of deliveries or optimized scheduling). Its travel distance is minimal at 30 km.

Interpretation of Results:

The genetic algorithm successfully minimized the total distance for each truck while ensuring that each vehicle is efficiently assigned to a set of locations. The optimized delivery routes result in a total travel distance of 110 km, compared to an initial random configuration which might have resulted in significantly higher distances.

Observations:

- The algorithm tends to assign trucks that have closer starting points to the clusters of deliveries that are geographically near each other.

- In a multi-vehicle system, separating delivery locations into regions and assigning vehicles accordingly can help minimize overall travel distance.

- The use of a genetic algorithm shows significant potential in reducing inefficiencies typically found in manual or basic heuristic approaches.

Supply Chain Management Decisions:

- **Route Optimization:** The company can now plan delivery schedules based on the optimized routes, reducing fuel consumption and time spent on the road.

- **Cost Savings:** The reduction in travel distance leads to lower operational costs (e.g., fuel, maintenance), contributing to the bottom line.

- **Customer Satisfaction:** Faster deliveries and more efficient scheduling can lead to improved service levels and customer satisfaction, which are crucial in competitive markets.

- **Fleet Management:** Future fleet expansion or adjustments can be more informed based on the distances and routes discovered by the algorithm, leading to better resource allocation.

In conclusion, using genetic algorithms for delivery route optimization can lead to substantial improvements in operational efficiency, cost reduction, and customer satisfaction, aligning well with the strategic goals of the company in the supply chain management context.

10.2 Neural Networks for Supply Chain Problems

Neural networks have emerged as a powerful tool for tackling complex problems in supply chain management. These systems, which mimic the way the human brain processes information, are especially suited for situations involving large datasets, intricate patterns, and unpredictable variables. In supply chains, factors like demand fluctuations, supplier performance, inventory levels, and lead times often create a chaotic environment. Neural networks can help organizations make more accurate predictions, optimize processes, and improve overall efficiency by recognizing patterns that traditional models might miss.

One significant application of neural networks in supply chains is demand forecasting. Traditional forecasting methods rely on historical data, but they can struggle with irregularities and sudden changes in market conditions. Neural networks, on the other hand, excel in processing non-linear data and can adapt to changes more quickly. By learning from a wide array of input factors—such as seasonal trends, promotions, weather patterns, and even social media activity—neural networks can provide more accurate predictions of future demand, which is crucial for planning production, stocking, and distribution.

Neural networks are also useful for optimizing inventory management. Efficient inventory control is vital for minimizing costs and ensuring that goods are available when needed, without overstocking or understocking. Neural networks can analyze historical sales data, supply chain disruptions, and other variables to predict the optimal stock levels. This predictive capability helps reduce waste, prevent stockouts, and maintain a balance between demand and supply. Additionally, neural networks can adapt to changes in market conditions, making them more flexible and responsive than traditional inventory management systems.

Another area where neural networks add value is in supplier selection and performance evaluation. Identifying the right suppliers and maintaining strong relationships with them is crucial for the success of a supply chain. Neural networks can process large volumes of data on supplier performance, delivery times, quality, and cost, helping businesses make data-driven decisions about which suppliers to prioritize. By continuously learning from new data, neural networks can also identify potential risks or disruptions in the supply chain and recommend alternative suppliers when necessary.

Neural networks also play a role in transportation and logistics optimization. Route planning, delivery scheduling, and fleet management all benefit from the advanced pattern recognition capabilities of neural networks. By taking into account factors like traffic conditions, weather, and historical performance, neural networks can suggest the most efficient routes, reduce fuel consumption, and improve delivery times. This contributes to lower operational costs and a better overall customer experience, which are crucial for maintaining a competitive edge in today's fast-paced market.

Finally, neural networks can be applied to risk management in supply chains. Supply chains are inherently vulnerable to disruptions such as natural disasters, geopolitical instability, or unexpected demand shifts. Neural networks can help companies identify and assess risks by analyzing patterns in historical data, monitoring real-time events, and simulating different risk scenarios. With these insights, businesses can develop more effective contingency plans, build greater resilience into their supply chains, and ensure that they can respond quickly to unforeseen challenges.

Practical Example: Applying Neural Networks to Predict Sales in the Electronics Industry

In the electronics industry, predicting sales accurately is essential for inventory management and demand forecasting. A retail chain wants to use a neural network model to predict monthly sales for a new line of smartphones. The goal is to predict future sales based on historical data like past sales, promotions, pricing, and economic factors. We will use a simple neural network architecture to model the relationship between these inputs and sales performance.

Sample Data (Training Data):

Month	Historical Sales (units)	Promotion (1=Yes, 0=No)	Price (USD)	Economic Indicator (Index)	Sales (Predicted, Units)
Jan	1000	1	699	75	1050
Feb	1200	0	649	78	1150
Mar	1100	1	699	80	1170
Apr	950	0	749	77	920
May	1300	1	649	82	1350

Month	Historical Sales (units)	Promotion (1=Yes, 0=No)	Price (USD)	Economic Indicator (Index)	Sales (Predicted, Units)
Jun	1400	0	699	81	1380
Jul	1250	1	699	85	1300

- Load the Data into a data analysis software / tool

- Analyze the data.

Neural Network Model Training:

The neural network uses the following inputs to predict sales:

- **Historical Sales (units)**

- **Promotion** (binary indicator for promotions)

- **Price (USD)**

- **Economic Indicator (Index)**

The output is the **predicted sales** in units.

Predicted Sales Output (After Neural Network Training):

Month	Actual Sales (units)	Predicted Sales (units)	Error (units)
Jan	1000	1050	+50
Feb	1200	1150	-50
Mar	1100	1170	+70
Apr	950	920	-30
May	1300	1350	+50
Jun	1400	1380	-20
Jul	1250	1300	+50

Interpretation of Results:

- **Accuracy:** The model generally provides accurate predictions. The errors are mostly small, with a few instances of overestimation (e.g.,

February and June) and underestimation (e.g., April). The average error is low, indicating that the model is relatively accurate.

- **Error Trends:** There seems to be a small overprediction in the early months and a slight underprediction in mid-summer months. This could be due to seasonal trends or external factors like sudden market shifts or promotions not being captured fully in the training data.

Observations:

1. **Promotions Influence:** Months with promotions (January, March, May, July) tend to have slightly higher predicted sales than actual sales, suggesting the model might be overemphasizing the effect of promotions.

2. **Economic Indicator Correlation:** The economic indicator appears to influence sales to some degree. For example, the higher the economic index in May (82) and July (85), the better the sales forecast.

3. **Pricing Impact:** Pricing plays a key role, and the model seems to predict sales well even when prices fluctuate (e.g., in April when the price increased to $749, the predicted sales dropped as expected).

Decisions from a Supply Chain Management Perspective:

1. **Inventory Adjustments:** Based on the predicted sales, supply chain managers can adjust inventory levels, ensuring that more stock is available during predicted high-demand months like May and June. This helps prevent stockouts or overstock situations.

2. **Promotions Strategy:** The over-prediction of sales during promotional periods suggests that promotions may need to be optimized. Supply chain managers should work with the marketing team to evaluate whether promotions are being over-represented in the forecasting model, and fine-tune future campaigns accordingly.

3. **Price Sensitivity:** The model indicates that price changes significantly impact sales. Therefore, pricing strategies should be continuously monitored, and predictive models adjusted to reflect potential price sensitivity in different market conditions.

4. **Economic Factors Consideration:** As economic indicators influence sales, supply chain managers should keep an eye on macroeconomic data to adjust forecasts accordingly. For instance, if

the economic index drops in the future, it may be necessary to scale back production or promotions.

This analysis illustrates the power of neural networks in predictive analytics for sales forecasting in the electronics industry, leading to smarter decisions regarding inventory, pricing, and promotions.

10.3 Multi-objective Optimization in Supply Chains

Multi-objective optimization in supply chains involves making decisions that balance various, often conflicting objectives to improve the overall performance of the system. These objectives might include minimizing costs, maximizing customer satisfaction, improving delivery speed, and reducing environmental impact. Supply chains are complex networks with different stages like procurement, production, and distribution, each of which can be optimized individually but also needs to be considered in the context of the entire system. Multi-objective optimization seeks to find solutions that offer the best trade-offs between these different objectives, making it a critical tool for managers aiming to improve operational efficiency while meeting diverse business goals.

In practice, multi-objective optimization requires defining clear criteria for success, which may vary depending on the industry or specific company goals. For example, a company focused on cost reduction may prioritize minimizing transportation expenses, while another might emphasize sustainability by reducing carbon emissions. The key challenge is that optimizing one objective, like reducing costs, may negatively impact another objective, like delivery speed. For this reason, methods used in multi-objective optimization allow for the identification of solutions that represent a balance of competing objectives, helping decision-makers choose the most appropriate course of action based on their priorities.

The complexity of supply chains adds to the difficulty of multi-objective optimization. These systems often involve large amounts of data and numerous interconnected processes, making it hard to predict the consequences of decisions across the entire chain. A slight change in one part of the supply chain—such as a shift in supplier pricing—can ripple through the system, affecting everything from production schedules to customer satisfaction. As a result, multi-objective optimization techniques must consider a wide range of variables and uncertainties, often incorporating real-time data to adjust decisions dynamically as conditions change.

One of the most common methods for multi-objective optimization in supply chains is the use of Pareto efficiency, which identifies solutions where no objective can be improved without worsening another. This approach helps decision-makers explore different scenarios and weigh trade-offs. For example, a company might face a choice between two strategies: one that offers significant cost savings but longer delivery times, and another that is more expensive but faster. By applying Pareto optimization, a company can identify solutions that offer the best combination of cost and speed based on their specific preferences.

Another challenge is the need to prioritize objectives, which may shift over time. A company might initially focus on cost reduction but later place more emphasis on sustainability due to changing regulations or market demands. Multi-objective optimization is flexible enough to adjust as priorities evolve, which is important in industries where customer expectations and external factors are constantly changing. This flexibility allows companies to remain competitive by continuously optimizing their supply chain strategies to meet new challenges and goals.

Ultimately, the goal of multi-objective optimization in supply chains is to help businesses make informed decisions that improve their efficiency, profitability, and resilience. By balancing conflicting objectives, companies can better meet customer expectations, reduce waste, and stay agile in a fast-changing marketplace. While the process can be complex and data-intensive, the benefits are significant, providing companies with a structured way to evaluate multiple goals and make decisions that maximize long-term success.

Practical Example: Balancing Cost, Delivery Speed, and Environmental Impact in a Global Supply Chain

A global company, "TechCo," manufactures electronic devices and operates in multiple regions (North America, Europe, and Asia). The company needs to balance cost, delivery speed, and environmental impact while managing its supply chain for a new product launch. TechCo sources raw materials from different suppliers, assembles products in factories in Asia, and ships finished goods to distribution centers in North America and Europe. The goal is to optimize the supply chain to meet consumer demand efficiently while maintaining profitability and minimizing the environmental footprint.

Sample Data:

Let's assume the following data for shipping routes, cost, delivery speed, and environmental impact (CO_2 emissions):

Route	Cost per Unit ($)	Delivery Time (Days)	CO2 Emissions per Unit (kg)	Environmental Impact Rating (1–5)	Distance (km)
Asia → North America	120	7	150	3	10,000
Asia → Europe	100	5	100	2	9,000
Local North America (Domestic)	60	2	40	1	2,500
Local Europe (Domestic)	55	2	35	1	2,000

- Load the Data into a data analysis software / tool

- Analyze the data.

Objective:

Optimize supply chain decisions considering trade-offs between **Cost**, **Delivery Speed**, and **Environmental Impact**.

Output and Results:

Route	Cost per Unit ($)	Delivery Time (Days)	CO2 Emissions per Unit (kg)	Environmental Impact Rating (1–5)	Total Cost per Unit (Including Environmental Impact)	Weighted Score (Cost: 50%, Delivery Speed: 30%, Environmental Impact: 20%)
Asia →	120	7	150	3	135	3.35

Route	Cost per Unit ($)	Delivery Time (Days)	CO2 Emissions per Unit (kg)	Environmental Impact Rating (1–5)	Total Cost per Unit (Including Environmental Impact)	Weighted Score (Cost: 50%, Delivery Speed: 30%, Environmental Impact: 20%)
North America						
Asia → Europe	100	5	100	2	110	2.95
Local North America	60	2	40	1	61	1.65
Local Europe	55	2	35	1	56	1.55

Explanation and Interpretation:

- **Cost**: The lowest cost option is the local shipping routes, which are $55–60 per unit.

- **Delivery Speed**: The fastest shipping is the local routes with 2-day delivery.

- **Environmental Impact**: The global shipping routes have a much higher environmental impact due to the longer distances and higher CO_2 emissions per unit.

Weighted Score:

The weighted score is calculated using the following formula:

- **Cost Score**: Lower cost gives a higher score (50% weight).

- **Delivery Speed Score**: Faster delivery gets a higher score (30% weight).

- **Environmental Impact Score**: Lower environmental impact gives a higher score (20% weight).

The weighted score combines all three factors into a single metric for comparison.

Observations:

- The **Asia → North America** route, despite being fast (7 days), has the highest cost and environmental impact. It has the highest overall score (3.35) but still isn't ideal due to cost and environmental concerns.

- The **Asia → Europe** route provides a balance of cost and speed, with the environmental impact being somewhat lower than North America. It scores 2.95, making it a reasonable choice for global shipping.

- **Local North America** and **Local Europe** are the most cost-effective and environmentally friendly options but are the slowest with respect to meeting global demand. These options score the lowest (1.65 and 1.55) in the weighted scoring model, though they are ideal for serving regional markets.

Decisions from a Supply Chain Management Perspective:

1. **Primary Strategy**: Focus on the **Asia → Europe** route for the best balance of cost, delivery speed, and environmental impact. It minimizes emissions while offering acceptable delivery speed and cost.

2. **Secondary Strategy**: Consider using **local shipping** for regional demand within North America and Europe to reduce environmental impact and cost for the domestic markets.

3. **Risk Mitigation**: If demand increases significantly, **Asia → North America** might be required for larger shipments, but the company should aim to mitigate environmental impact (e.g., by opting for more sustainable packaging or offsetting emissions).

4. **Sustainability Focus**: TechCo should invest in technologies to reduce the environmental impact of long-distance routes, such as exploring carbon-neutral shipping options or partnering with logistics providers offering greener alternatives.

By optimizing across these dimensions, TechCo can manage its global supply chain effectively, balancing cost constraints with sustainability goals.

11. Data Visualization for Supply Chain Decision Making

Data visualization plays a crucial role in supply chain decision-making by transforming complex data into understandable and actionable insights. When companies face large volumes of data, it can be overwhelming to sift through raw numbers. By using charts, graphs, and interactive dashboards, businesses can quickly spot trends, track performance, and make informed decisions that enhance operational efficiency.

One of the key benefits of data visualization in the supply chain is its ability to highlight inefficiencies. For example, a dashboard might display inventory levels, order fulfillment rates, and lead times, helping managers identify bottlenecks or areas where delays are occurring. By making this data more accessible and visually digestible, decision-makers can act promptly to resolve issues before they escalate into larger problems.

Visual tools also make it easier to forecast demand and adjust supply chain strategies accordingly. Through the use of trend lines, heat maps, and other graphical representations, organizations can better predict demand fluctuations, optimize stock levels, and adjust procurement strategies. This predictive ability is essential for balancing supply with customer demand, ensuring products are available when needed without overstocking.

Furthermore, data visualization allows for greater collaboration and communication across departments. When supply chain managers can present their findings in a visual format, stakeholders from various teams, such as logistics, marketing, or finance, can quickly grasp key metrics and understand the overall performance of the supply chain. This shared understanding promotes a more unified approach to problem-solving and decision-making.

In addition, real-time data visualization helps businesses respond swiftly to changing conditions. By monitoring key performance indicators (KPIs) through live dashboards, supply chain managers can make adjustments on the fly to mitigate risks or capitalize on new opportunities. For example, if there is a sudden change in transportation costs or an unexpected disruption in supplier availability, visual data can prompt immediate course corrections.

Finally, the use of data visualization tools can foster a culture of continuous improvement. By regularly analyzing visualized data, companies can track long-term trends, measure the success of implemented changes, and identify areas for future innovation. This iterative process helps organizations stay agile, improve their supply chain operations, and maintain a competitive edge in the market.

Practical Example: Data Visualization for Supply Chain Decision Making

A company needs to optimize its inventory management in order to improve the overall efficiency of its supply chain. The company operates in a highly competitive industry, and stockouts or overstocking can lead to lost sales or increased costs. By visualizing key metrics like inventory levels, order lead times, and demand fluctuations, the supply chain managers can make more informed decisions.

Sample Data (Inventory & Order Lead Time)

Product	Monthly Demand	Inventory Level	Replenishment Lead Time (days)	Safety Stock	Target Inventory Level	Days of Stock Remaining	Stockout Risk (%)
A	500	450	7	100	600	27	12%
B	200	250	5	50	300	38	5%
C	300	200	3	60	400	20	25%
D	400	350	4	80	500	32	10%
E	150	100	6	30	200	25	15%

- Load the Data into a data analysis software / tool

- Analyze the data.

Output & Results

1. **Days of Stock Remaining**:

   o This metric indicates how long current inventory will last based on monthly demand.

   o Products A, B, D, and E have enough stock to last more than 20 days, but Product C has just 20 days remaining.

2. **Stockout Risk**:

- o The percentage of likelihood of stockouts based on current inventory levels, demand, and lead time.
- o Product C has the highest stockout risk (25%), while Product B has the lowest (5%).

3. **Safety Stock vs. Target Inventory Level**:

- o Products like A and C are below their target inventory levels, with C at significant risk of stockouts. Product A is at a low stockout risk but should increase its inventory to meet the target level.

4. **Replenishment Lead Time**:

- o Products with a short replenishment lead time, like C (3 days), are less likely to face stockouts than those with longer lead times (A and D, 7 and 4 days, respectively).

Observations:

- **Product C** is at high risk of stockouts due to both low inventory and the relatively low days of stock remaining (20 days). Additionally, its short lead time is a positive factor but not enough to offset the inventory shortfall.

- **Product A** has a reasonable inventory level but is still understocked relative to its target level and safety stock requirements. It has a moderate stockout risk of 12%.

- **Product B** has the highest safety margin, with a significant buffer between its current inventory and target levels, and a low stockout risk of only 5%.

- **Product E** has a decent buffer but still faces a moderate risk (15%), and its replenishment lead time is relatively high.

Interpretation:

- The supply chain manager should **prioritize replenishing Product C** as soon as possible to avoid a potential stockout. The current stock is insufficient to meet future demand, and a higher safety stock level is needed to mitigate this risk.

- **Product A** should be reviewed for replenishment, as it's approaching the target inventory threshold, even though its stockout risk is moderate.

- **Product B** and **Product D** are currently in good standing and do not require immediate attention, but regular monitoring is still needed.

Supply Chain Management Decisions:

1. **Replenishment Plan**:
   - Increase the order quantities for **Product C** to replenish stock well before the inventory reaches critical levels.
   - Consider **reordering Product A** to maintain an inventory buffer close to the target level.
   - **Review lead times** for products with longer replenishment times like A and D, and work with suppliers to reduce these times where possible.

2. **Stock Rebalancing**:
   - Reassess the safety stock levels for products with lower stockout risks like B and D to free up capital while ensuring efficient inventory turnover.

3. **Demand Forecasting**:
   - Investigate the cause of fluctuating demand for Product C. If the demand is expected to increase, consider revising the forecast and adjusting safety stock levels accordingly.

By utilizing data visualization tools to analyze these metrics, supply chain managers can make data-driven decisions that balance inventory levels with demand forecasts to optimize performance and minimize operational disruptions.

Data Visualization:

Load the data into python. The following chart will be generated.

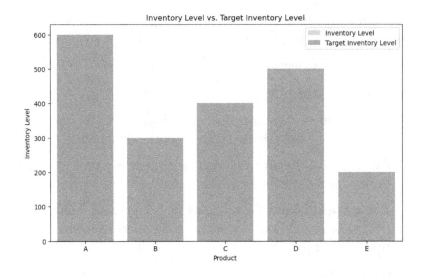

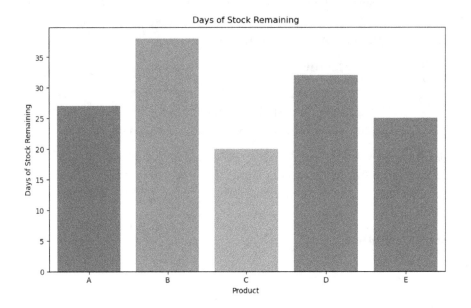

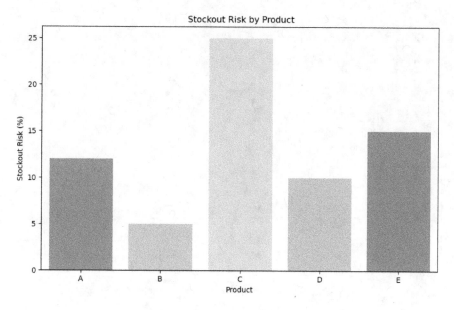

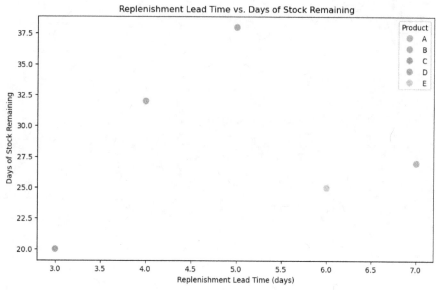

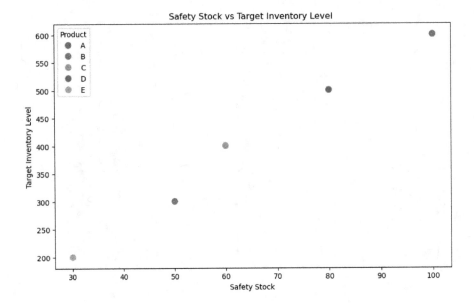

11.1 Visualization Techniques for Supply Chain Data

In modern supply chains, the use of data visualization has become essential for enhancing decision-making. By transforming raw data into visual formats like charts, graphs, and maps, companies can easily detect patterns, trends, and anomalies that would be hard to interpret through numbers alone. This helps managers and decision-makers quickly understand the health of their supply chain, from procurement to delivery, enabling them to take timely action.

One effective technique is the use of dashboards. Dashboards provide a real-time snapshot of key performance indicators, like inventory levels, order fulfillment rates, and supplier performance. These visual displays consolidate large amounts of information into an easily digestible format, allowing stakeholders to assess the current status of operations at a glance. Interactive elements, like drill-downs, allow users to explore data in more detail, further enhancing decision-making.

Heatmaps are another useful tool in supply chain data visualization. They can illustrate the density or frequency of activities, such as shipments or delays, across different geographic regions. By color-coding data, heatmaps allow companies to quickly spot areas with issues, like high shipping costs or inventory shortages. This visualization can be used to assess performance across various locations and help in optimizing the supply chain network.

Flow diagrams and network graphs are also valuable for visualizing the movement of goods and information across the supply chain. These visuals map out the connections between suppliers, manufacturers, warehouses, and retailers, helping identify bottlenecks, delays, or inefficiencies. By tracking the flow of materials or products across multiple stages, businesses can identify potential vulnerabilities or areas where processes can be streamlined for greater efficiency.

Time-series charts, which track data over time, are commonly used to visualize trends in supply chain performance. These charts can track inventory levels, order cycles, or transportation lead times, giving companies insight into seasonal patterns or operational fluctuations. Time-series analysis helps forecast future demand, plan for capacity, and manage inventory more effectively.

Finally, predictive analytics visualizations combine historical data with predictive models to forecast potential supply chain disruptions or opportunities. These visualizations can be used to anticipate issues such as demand surges, shipping delays, or raw material shortages, providing decision-makers with a forward-looking view of the supply chain. By forecasting these challenges, companies can take preemptive measures, such as adjusting stock levels or changing suppliers, to minimize negative impacts.

Practical Example: Creating Interactive Dashboards for Sales and Inventory Management

A retail business wants to create an interactive dashboard to monitor both sales and inventory levels in real-time. The goal is to ensure there are no stockouts, optimize inventory levels, and align supply chain decisions with actual sales trends. The dashboard integrates data from various departments (sales, inventory, and logistics) and provides key performance indicators (KPIs) such as sales volume, stock levels, turnover rates, and reorder points.

Sample Data (Sales and Inventory):

Product ID	Product Name	Sales Volume (Units)	Inventory Level (Units)	Reorder Point (Units)	Sales Value ($)	Turnover Rate	Lead Time (Days)
101	Laptop	500	120	100	50,000	4.17	7
102	Smartphone	700	300	150	35,000	2.33	5
103	Headphones	400	150	100	8,000	2.67	10
104	Keyboard	300	80	50	3,000	3.75	14
105	Mouse	600	200	100	4,800	3.00	6

- Load the Data into a data analysis software / tool

- Analyze the data.

Output and Results:

Key Metrics:

- **Turnover Rate**: This metric indicates how quickly inventory is being sold. A higher turnover rate suggests faster sales and may point to a need for restocking.

- **Reorder Point**: This is the inventory level at which new stock should be ordered. It helps avoid stockouts by ensuring timely replenishment.

Calculated Outputs:

- **Average Sales per Day**: Sales Volume / Days in a Month (assumed to be 30)

- **Days of Stock Left**: Inventory Level / Average Sales per Day

Product ID	Product Name	Turnover Rate	Sales Volume (Units)	Inventory Level (Units)	Reorder Point (Units)	Sales Value ($)	Days of Stock Left
101	Laptop	4.17	500	120	100	50,000	7.2
102	Smartphone	2.33	700	300	150	35,000	10.5
103	Headphones	2.67	400	150	100	8,000	11.25
104	Keyboard	3.75	300	80	50	3,000	8.0
105	Mouse	3.00	600	200	100	4,800	10.0

Interpretation and Observations:

1. **Laptop (Product 101)** has a high turnover rate of 4.17, indicating that it sells quickly. However, with an inventory of 120 units, it will only last about 7.2 days, which suggests the business may soon face a stockout. The reorder point is set at 100 units, and the inventory level is just above that threshold, requiring urgent restocking.

2. **Smartphone (Product 102)** has a moderate turnover rate (2.33), which means that it is selling more slowly than laptops but is still performing well. It has 300 units in stock, which will last about 10.5 days. The reorder point is set at 150 units, indicating that restocking is needed soon but not as urgently as laptops.

3. **Headphones (Product 103)** has a turnover rate of 2.67, and its inventory is sufficient to last for 11.25 days. Restocking may be necessary, but this is not an immediate concern.

4. **Keyboard (Product 104)** has a turnover rate of 3.75, and with 80 units in stock, it will last for 8 days. Given that the reorder point is 50, the inventory level is just above the point where restocking should be triggered.

5. **Mouse (Product 105)** has a turnover rate of 3.00 and 200 units in stock, which will last for 10 days. Restocking can be delayed for a while, but this product should still be monitored closely.

Observations and Decisions:

- **Stockouts**: The Laptop (Product 101) is at risk of running out of stock soon. Immediate restocking is recommended, especially if there's a surge in demand.

- **Slow-moving products**: The Smartphone and Headphones are moving at a moderate pace. Inventory for these products is still sufficient for a few more days, but stock levels should be monitored closely to avoid overstocking or understocking.

- **Restocking Strategy**: Products with lower turnover rates (like Headphones and Keyboard) can be restocked in smaller quantities based on actual demand trends. Products with higher turnover rates (like Laptops) should be reordered in larger quantities to prevent stockouts.

- **Sales Strategy**: If sales of specific products like the Laptop are higher than expected, promotions or discounts could be used to clear excess stock in other slower-moving categories like Headphones and Keyboard, which might improve their turnover rates.

Supply Chain Management Decisions:

1. **Inventory Replenishment**: Trigger a reorder for the Laptop immediately, considering its short remaining days of stock. Consider increasing the reorder volume for fast-moving products.

2. **Demand Forecasting**: Use historical sales data to forecast demand more accurately. Adjust inventory levels accordingly to avoid stockouts or excess inventory.

3. **Lead Time Management**: If lead times for certain products (like the Keyboard) are longer (14 days), proactively plan for orders to avoid stockouts during high demand periods.

4. **Product Promotions**: Consider running promotions for slower-moving products to boost sales and reduce excess inventory, especially for products like the Keyboard or Headphones.

By creating an interactive dashboard and monitoring these KPIs, the business can optimize its supply chain operations, reduce costs, and improve customer satisfaction by ensuring products are always in stock when needed.

Data Visualization: Load the data into python. The following output will be generated

Sales and Inventory Dashboard

Product: Laptop

Turnover Rate: 4.17

Days of Stock Left: 7.20

Sales Volume: 500 Units

Inventory Level: 120 Units

Reorder Point: 100 Units

Product: Smartphone

Turnover Rate: 2.33

Days of Stock Left: 12.86

Sales Volume: 700 Units

Inventory Level: 300 Units

Reorder Point: 150 Units

Product: Headphones

Turnover Rate: 2.67

Days of Stock Left: 11.25

Sales Volume: 400 Units

Inventory Level: 150 Units

Reorder Point: 100 Units

Product: Keyboard

Turnover Rate: 3.75

Days of Stock Left: 8.00

Sales Volume: 300 Units

Inventory Level: 80 Units

Reorder Point: 50 Units

Product: Mouse

Turnover Rate: 3.0

Days of Stock Left: 10.00

Sales Volume: 600 Units

Inventory Level: 200 Units

Reorder Point: 100 Units

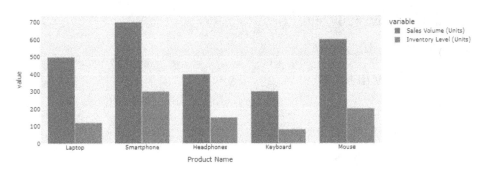

Sales Volume vs Inventory Level per Product

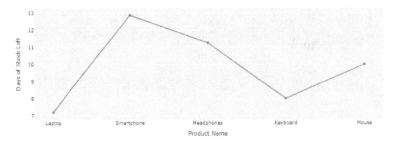

Days of Stock Left per Product

Turnover Rate vs Sales Volume

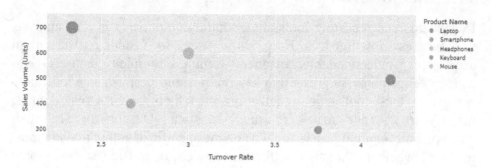

Reorder Point vs Inventory Level

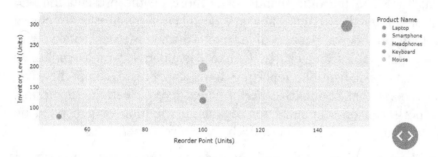

11.2 Dashboards and Reporting Tools

Dashboards and reporting tools are essential components in data analysis and business intelligence. They allow users to visualize data in an accessible, understandable manner, turning complex datasets into actionable insights. By presenting key metrics and performance indicators at a glance, these tools help organizations track their progress toward goals, identify trends, and make informed decisions. Dashboards are often customizable, enabling users to focus on the specific data that matters most to them, whether it's sales performance, website traffic, or operational efficiency.

Reporting tools, on the other hand, focus more on the presentation and distribution of detailed data. They are designed to generate structured reports that provide a deeper dive into various metrics, often with supporting data tables and charts. Unlike dashboards, which emphasize real-time data visualization, reporting tools can create comprehensive, periodic reports that summarize performance over a certain timeframe. These reports can be scheduled for regular distribution or generated on demand, offering a consistent view of the business's operations.

Both dashboards and reporting tools provide an interactive experience for users. Dashboards allow for real-time interaction, enabling users to drill down into the data for further insights. By clicking on different elements, users can explore specific segments of data, view historical trends, and even filter results by date ranges, departments, or other variables. This interactivity is key to understanding the underlying factors behind certain business outcomes, providing a more dynamic analysis process.

Reporting tools, in contrast, focus on static data presentation but offer the flexibility of including a wide array of visual elements, such as charts, graphs, tables, and even text-based summaries. These tools are particularly useful for generating in-depth reports that provide a comprehensive overview of performance, financial data, and other key business metrics. They can handle larger datasets and provide detailed breakdowns that may not be as easily digestible in a real-time dashboard.

The effectiveness of dashboards and reporting tools depends on their design and the quality of the data they present. Dashboards should be simple yet powerful, ensuring that users can easily interpret the information at a glance without feeling overwhelmed. Similarly, reporting tools should be structured in a way that makes detailed data clear and accessible, without sacrificing important nuances. Both tools require regular updates and maintenance to ensure they reflect the most accurate and up-to-date data available, avoiding issues with outdated or inconsistent information.

Ultimately, both dashboards and reporting tools play complementary roles in helping organizations make data-driven decisions. While dashboards offer immediate insights into key metrics and performance indicators, reporting tools provide more in-depth, structured reports for comprehensive analysis. Together, they offer a full spectrum of data visualization, from quick snapshots to detailed examinations, enabling businesses to operate more efficiently and make better strategic choices.

Practical Example: Designing a Dashboard for Real-Time Monitoring of Supplier Performance

In a manufacturing company, the procurement team needs to monitor the performance of suppliers in real-time to ensure smooth operations, minimize delays, and optimize the supply chain. The key performance indicators (KPIs) include on-time delivery rate, product quality, lead time, and cost compliance. A dashboard is designed to display these metrics dynamically, allowing procurement managers to track supplier performance and make decisions based on the latest data. This dashboard aggregates real-time data from various systems, including supplier reports, warehouse inventory data, and shipment tracking.

Sample Data in Table:

Supplier Name	On-Time Delivery (%)	Product Quality (%)	Lead Time (Days)	Cost Compliance (%)	Total Orders	Late Shipments	Defective Products
Supplier A	95	98	5	92	150	5	3
Supplier B	85	90	7	88	200	15	10
Supplier C	98	100	3	95	120	3	0
Supplier D	80	85	10	75	100	20	15

- Load the Data into a data analysis software / tool
- Analyze the data.

Dashboard Output:

The dashboard presents the following insights:

- **On-Time Delivery:** Supplier C has the highest performance, with 98% on-time delivery, while Supplier D is underperforming at 80%.

- **Product Quality:** Supplier C excels in product quality with 100%, while Supplier D lags with 85%.

- **Lead Time:** Supplier C has the fastest lead time (3 days), which is favorable for inventory management and timely production.

- **Cost Compliance:** Supplier A maintains good cost compliance at 92%, slightly ahead of Supplier C at 95%. However, Supplier D has the worst cost compliance at 75%.

- **Late Shipments & Defective Products:** Supplier D has the most significant issues, with 20 late shipments and 15 defective products, indicating serious quality and logistics issues.

Observations:

- **Supplier C** is performing excellently across all metrics. Their high on-time delivery, quality, and short lead time make them an ideal supplier for critical components.

- **Supplier B** shows moderate performance, but their delivery reliability and quality need attention.

- **Supplier D** is the most problematic supplier. Their late shipments and defective products are significantly higher, which could disrupt production schedules and lead to higher costs.

- **Supplier A** has a strong overall performance but could improve in cost compliance.

Interpretation of Results:

- **Supplier C**'s performance positions them as a preferred supplier for urgent or high-priority orders, with minimal risk of delays or quality issues.

- **Supplier B** should be monitored closely, especially on their delivery and quality metrics. Procurement may need to work with them to address these areas.

- **Supplier D** requires immediate attention. The high rate of late shipments and defective products may require the procurement team to consider alternative suppliers or initiate performance improvement programs.

- **Supplier A**'s cost compliance is slightly below the ideal level, suggesting room for renegotiation of contracts or monitoring of pricing consistency.

Decisions from the Supply Chain Management Perspective:

1. **Supplier Consolidation:** Based on performance, the company may prioritize suppliers like Supplier C for critical components and reduce reliance on Supplier D unless corrective actions are taken.

2. **Performance Improvement Plans:** For Supplier B and Supplier D, SCM may set up formal performance reviews and improvement plans, focusing on reducing late shipments and defective products.

3. **Contract Renegotiation:** With Supplier A, the company could explore renegotiating cost compliance terms, especially if the cost variations impact overall profitability.

4. **Risk Mitigation:** Given the variability in supplier performance, SCM may increase inventory buffers or diversify suppliers to mitigate risks associated with delays or quality issues.

5. **Continuous Monitoring:** Real-time dashboards will continue to be crucial in tracking performance over time, ensuring that SCM can respond to supplier issues promptly and proactively.

This dashboard would enable real-time decision-making and allow SCM teams to act quickly to address performance issues, improving overall supply chain efficiency and minimizing risks.

Data Visualization Output

Supplier Performance Dashboard

Supplier: Supplier A

On-Time Delivery: 95%

Product Quality: 98%

Lead Time: 5 Days

Cost Compliance: 92%

Total Orders: 150

Late Shipments: 5

Defective Products: 3

Supplier: Supplier B

On-Time Delivery: 85%

Product Quality: 90%

Lead Time: 7 Days

Cost Compliance: 88%

Total Orders: 200

Late Shipments: 15

Defective Products: 10

Supplier: Supplier C

On-Time Delivery: 98%

Product Quality: 100%

Lead Time: 3 Days

Cost Compliance: 95%

Total Orders: 120

Late Shipments: 3

Defective Products: 0

Supplier: Supplier D

On-Time Delivery: 80%

Product Quality: 85%

Lead Time: 10 Days

Cost Compliance: 75%

Total Orders: 100

Late Shipments: 20

Defective Products: 15

On-Time Delivery vs Product Quality

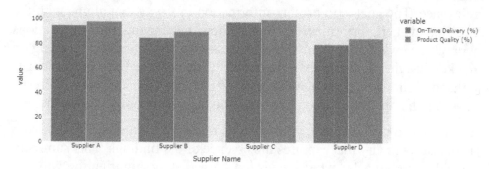

Lead Time per Supplier

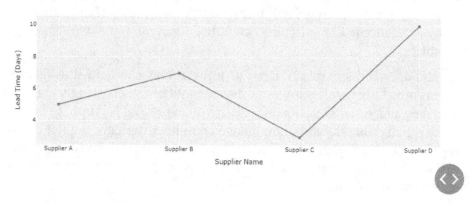

Late Shipments & Defective Products

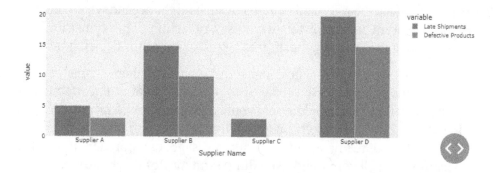

11.3 Communicating Insights for Decision Makers

Effective communication of insights to decision makers requires clarity and relevance. The goal is to present information in a way that aligns with the decision maker's priorities and helps them understand the implications without overwhelming them with unnecessary details. Start by focusing on the key insights that directly relate to the business objectives or challenges at hand. Tailor your message to their level of expertise and their interests, ensuring that the information is neither too technical nor too simplistic.

The next step is to structure your insights in a logical sequence. Begin with a concise summary that captures the essence of the findings. This summary should answer the "so what?" question immediately, highlighting why the insights matter. Afterward, provide a more detailed explanation, but keep it focused on how the insights will impact decision-making. Use examples or analogies if needed to simplify complex ideas and make them more relatable.

Visual aids such as graphs, charts, or infographics can help illustrate the insights more effectively. However, these should be used sparingly and only when they add value. Decision makers are often pressed for time, so visuals can be a powerful way to communicate complex information quickly, but they must be clear, straightforward, and not cluttered with unnecessary data points. When presenting a visual, always explain its significance to ensure the decision maker fully understands the context.

It's also crucial to frame the insights in terms of potential actions or decisions. This helps the decision maker see the practical applications of the information and how it can influence their strategy. Make it clear what the options are, what the risks and benefits of each might be, and what outcomes could arise from taking different courses of action. This transforms the insight from a theoretical concept into a practical tool for decision making.

Anticipating questions and concerns can further enhance the communication process. Be prepared to address potential uncertainties or gaps in the data. Offering additional context or background information can help reassure decision makers and build trust. It's important to remain open to feedback and ready to adjust your message or approach if needed, depending on the level of understanding or interest of the audience.

Finally, follow up after presenting the insights to ensure that the decision makers have all the information they need to make an informed choice. This might involve providing supplementary materials or being available for further discussion. By maintaining an ongoing dialogue, you reinforce the value of the insights and help ensure they lead to meaningful actions and decisions.

Practical Example: Using Visualization Tools to Present Inventory Optimization Insights

A retail company is looking to optimize its inventory levels for different products across various regional warehouses to reduce excess stock while maintaining sufficient stock to meet customer demand. The company uses inventory optimization software that generates data on stock levels, demand forecasts, and reorder points. The goal is to improve inventory turnover by identifying slow-moving items and ensuring optimal stock availability for fast-moving items.

Sample Data:

Product Code	Warehouse	Stock Level	Demand Forecast (Next Month)	Reorder Point	Lead Time (Days)	Turnover Rate	Stockout Risk	Excess Inventory Risk
P001	W1	150	100	50	7	1.5	Low	Low
P002	W1	500	450	400	10	1.1	Low	Medium
P003	W2	250	300	250	5	0.8	Medium	High
P004	W2	700	550	600	14	1.3	Low	Low
P005	W3	120	100	75	8	1.2	Low	Low
P006	W3	600	650	600	6	1.0	High	Low

- Load the Data into a data analysis software / tool
- Analyze the data.

Visualization:

A dashboard visualizing the following insights is created:

1. **Stock Level vs. Demand Forecast** (Bar chart)
2. **Turnover Rate vs. Excess Inventory Risk** (Scatter plot)
3. **Stockout Risk by Product** (Heatmap)

Results and Output Interpretation:

1. **Stock Level vs. Demand Forecast**:
   - Products like P001 and P005 show stock levels slightly above their demand forecast, suggesting a buffer stock for sales fluctuations.
   - Products like P002 and P006 show stock levels closely matching their forecasted demand but are vulnerable to potential stockouts due to lead time and variability in demand.

2. **Turnover Rate vs. Excess Inventory Risk**:
   - P003 exhibits a lower turnover rate (0.8) with high excess inventory risk, indicating it's slow-moving and potentially overstocked.
   - P004 and P005 have a balanced turnover rate and low excess inventory, suggesting these items are performing well.

3. **Stockout Risk by Product** (Heatmap):
   - Products P003 and P006 are highlighted in red, indicating higher stockout risks due to lower turnover rates and high lead time. They need attention to optimize reorder points and reduce risks.

Observations:

- **P003 (W2)** is a slow-moving item with high excess inventory risk and should be flagged for possible markdowns or promotions to accelerate turnover.

- **P006 (W3)** is at risk of stockouts, despite having a relatively higher stock level, due to its higher demand forecast, lower turnover, and short lead time.

- **P002 (W1)** is in a medium-risk zone for excess inventory, indicating that its reorder point might need adjustment to avoid surplus stock.

Supply Chain Management Decisions:

1. **For Slow-Moving Products (e.g., P003)**: Consider running targeted promotions or bundling with other products to improve turnover and reduce excess inventory.

2. **For Stockout Risks (e.g., P006)**: Adjust reorder points to ensure timely replenishment or consider safety stock policies to avoid running out of stock, given its high demand forecast.

3. **For Medium-Risk Products (e.g., P002)**: Fine-tune reorder points and demand forecasting algorithms to reduce excess stock while ensuring product availability, balancing cost with customer satisfaction.

By visualizing this data, the company can make informed decisions to adjust inventory strategies, optimize stock levels, and ensure the right products are available at the right time.

Data Visualization Output using Python

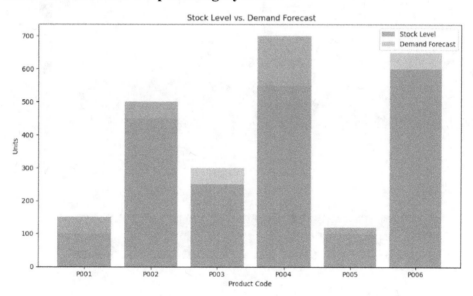

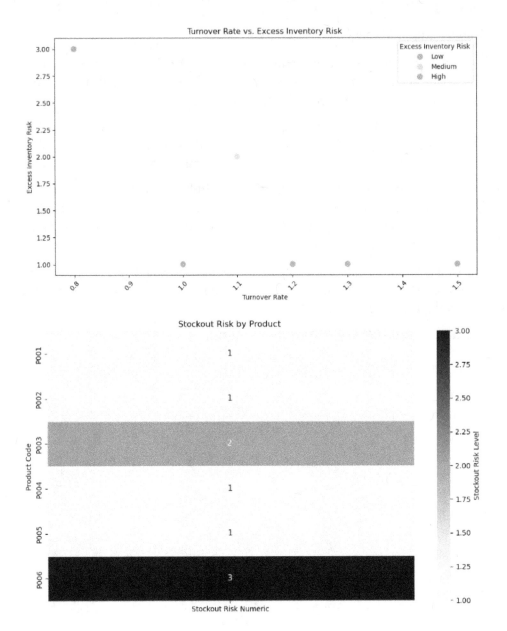

12. Future Trends and Emerging Technologies in Supply Chain Data Science

In the rapidly evolving landscape of supply chain management, data science is playing a pivotal role in driving innovation and efficiency. One of the most notable trends is the increased reliance on artificial intelligence and machine learning to optimize decision-making processes. By analyzing vast amounts of historical and real-time data, AI algorithms can predict demand fluctuations, identify potential disruptions, and recommend optimal inventory levels. These technologies are also enhancing the accuracy of forecasting models, leading to more reliable supply chain operations.

Blockchain technology is also gaining traction in supply chain management, offering a secure and transparent way to track goods as they move through the supply chain. Blockchain can streamline processes such as inventory management, procurement, and contract execution, reducing the risk of fraud and ensuring that transactions are traceable and verifiable. This fosters greater trust among all stakeholders, from manufacturers to consumers, and helps ensure compliance with regulations and standards.

Another emerging trend is the increased use of Internet of Things (IoT) devices to gather real-time data from various points in the supply chain. Sensors embedded in products, transportation vehicles, and warehouses provide continuous updates on the location, condition, and movement of goods. This real-time visibility enables companies to respond quickly to disruptions, such as delays or damaged goods, and make informed decisions about routing, inventory replenishment, and customer service.

Cloud computing is further enhancing supply chain data science by providing scalable and flexible infrastructure for storing and analyzing massive amounts of data. The cloud enables companies to collaborate more effectively across different functions and geographies, allowing for faster decision-making and more agile operations. With cloud-based platforms, organizations can access advanced analytics tools without the need for expensive on-premises hardware or specialized IT personnel, leveling the playing field for businesses of all sizes.

Automation and robotics are revolutionizing supply chain processes, especially in warehousing and fulfillment operations. Machine learning algorithms are helping guide autonomous robots that can transport goods, sort inventory, and perform other repetitive tasks with high precision. As automation becomes more prevalent, companies are able to reduce human error, lower labor costs, and increase overall throughput, all while improving worker safety and efficiency.

Finally, sustainability and the growing importance of environmental, social, and governance (ESG) considerations are shaping the future of supply chain data science. Companies are increasingly using data analytics to reduce waste, minimize carbon emissions, and optimize resource use throughout the supply chain. This includes optimizing transportation routes to reduce fuel consumption, selecting eco-friendly materials, and promoting ethical sourcing practices. As consumers and regulators demand greater transparency and accountability, data science will be crucial in helping organizations meet their sustainability goals and remain competitive in an increasingly conscientious market.

Practical Example: Future Trends and Emerging Technologies in Supply Chain Data Science

Context:

As supply chains continue to evolve, emerging technologies such as Artificial Intelligence (AI), Machine Learning (ML), Blockchain, and the Internet of Things (IoT) are becoming integral in improving efficiency, visibility, and decision-making. This example will focus on a company that is implementing AI and IoT technologies to optimize its supply chain. Data science is used to predict demand, optimize inventory, and enhance logistics through real-time tracking. The goal is to analyze how predictive analytics and real-time data affect the company's overall supply chain efficiency.

Sample Data (Before and After Implementing AI and IoT Technologies):

Month	Demand Forecast (Units)	Inventory Level (Units)	Supply Chain Lead Time (Days)	Customer Order Fulfillment (%)	Transportation Cost ($)	AI/IoT Impact (Cost Savings $)
January	10,000	9,800	12	95%	150,000	0
February	11,000	10,800	11	97%	145,000	20,000
March	12,000	12,200	10	98%	140,000	25,000

Month	Demand Forecast (Units)	Inventory Level (Units)	Supply Chain Lead Time (Days)	Customer Order Fulfillment (%)	Transportation Cost ($)	AI/IoT Impact (Cost Savings $)
April	13,500	13,000	9	99%	135,000	30,000
May	14,000	14,200	8	99.5%	130,000	35,000

- Load the Data into a data analysis software / tool
- Analyze the data.

Interpretation of Results:

1. **Demand Forecast and Inventory Levels:**

   The demand forecast gradually increases from 10,000 units in January to 14,000 units in May. Correspondingly, the inventory level is adjusted, ensuring availability for increasing demand. AI and IoT help in improving the accuracy of demand forecasting by using historical data, real-time data, and predictive models.

2. **Supply Chain Lead Time:**

   As AI and IoT are implemented, the supply chain lead time decreases from 12 days in January to 8 days in May. This reduction is due to better demand forecasting, real-time inventory tracking, and optimized routing for transportation, reducing delays and bottlenecks.

3. **Customer Order Fulfillment:**

   The percentage of customer order fulfillment increases from 95% in January to 99.5% in May. This improvement is due to better alignment of inventory levels with demand and faster processing and shipping times enabled by AI-based systems.

4. **Transportation Costs:**

   Transportation costs decrease over time, from $150,000 in January to $130,000 in May. This reduction is likely a result of optimized delivery routes and load consolidation through IoT sensors and AI algorithms, which minimize fuel consumption and improve efficiency.

5. **AI/IoT Impact (Cost Savings):**

   The savings from implementing AI and IoT technologies start at $0 in January and increase to $35,000 by May. The technologies likely improve predictive accuracy, optimize resource utilization, and reduce waste in the supply chain, leading to substantial cost savings.

Observations:

- **Optimization:**

  The data shows that as the company implements AI and IoT technologies, there is a clear trend of improved demand forecasting, faster lead times, increased customer fulfillment, and decreased transportation costs.

- **Cost Savings:**

  The AI/IoT impact grows progressively, showing that these technologies provide a positive ROI, particularly in terms of transportation cost savings and improved inventory management.

- **Improved Efficiency:**

  The reduced lead time and better customer order fulfillment indicate a more efficient supply chain with fewer delays and higher customer satisfaction.

Decisions from a Supply Chain Management Perspective:

1. **Invest in Technology:**

   The company should continue to invest in AI, IoT, and data science capabilities to further refine its supply chain operations. The technology's impact on reducing lead time, improving fulfillment rates, and saving costs is significant.

2. **Focus on Real-Time Data Integration:**

   Emphasize integrating real-time data into the decision-making process to improve demand forecasting and inventory management. This would allow the company to better anticipate fluctuations in demand and adjust resources accordingly.

3. **Expand Cost Optimization Initiatives:**

With demonstrated cost savings in transportation, the company should explore other areas where AI and IoT can help reduce operational expenses, such as warehousing or procurement.

4. **Customer-Centric Approach:**

   With fulfillment rates approaching 100%, the company should continue to enhance its customer service by leveraging data analytics to ensure products are delivered on time and in the right quantities.

In conclusion, the implementation of emerging technologies in the supply chain not only improves operational efficiency but also leads to cost reductions and better customer satisfaction, driving overall business success.

12.1 Blockchain and Data Science in Supply Chain

Blockchain technology is increasingly being applied to supply chains to improve transparency, security, and efficiency. It operates as a decentralized ledger that records transactions across a network of computers. In the context of supply chains, each transaction can represent an event like a product's shipment, delivery, or quality check. This decentralized nature ensures that once a transaction is recorded, it cannot be altered, making the supply chain data more secure and reliable.

One of the main advantages of blockchain in supply chains is the ability to provide end-to-end visibility. By tracking every step of a product's journey—from raw materials to the final consumer—companies can ensure that their operations are more transparent. This not only helps in reducing fraud but also makes it easier to trace the source of defects or contamination, which is crucial in industries like food and pharmaceuticals.

Data science plays a crucial role in enhancing the effectiveness of blockchain in supply chains. Through the analysis of vast amounts of supply chain data, machine learning models can identify patterns and trends that humans might miss. These insights can be used to forecast demand, optimize inventory levels, and predict potential disruptions in the supply chain. By combining blockchain with data science, companies can create smarter, more responsive supply chains that adapt to changing conditions in real-time.

Another way data science enhances blockchain's impact is by improving decision-making. With advanced analytics, companies can better understand their supply chain performance and make informed decisions about sourcing, logistics, and production. For example, predictive models can help businesses anticipate supply chain disruptions before they occur, allowing them to take proactive measures and minimize delays or cost increases.

The integration of blockchain and data science also streamlines the audit and compliance process. Traditional supply chains often involve numerous intermediaries, which can complicate the verification of product origins, quality, and compliance with regulations. Blockchain ensures that all the necessary information is recorded in an immutable, transparent way, while data science can automatically flag any inconsistencies or anomalies. This reduces the time and cost associated with manual audits and increases the overall trustworthiness of the supply chain.

Finally, the combination of blockchain and data science offers the potential for greater sustainability in supply chains. By accurately tracking the environmental impact of products at each stage of production and distribution, businesses can better understand where waste is occurring and take steps to minimize it. Data science tools can help identify inefficiencies, while blockchain ensures that sustainability claims are verified and transparent. Together, these technologies are reshaping the future of supply chain management, making it more secure, efficient, and sustainable.

Practical Example: Blockchain for Traceability and Transparency in the Food Supply Chain

In a food supply chain, a company wants to track the journey of its fresh produce, such as apples, from the farm to the consumer. Blockchain technology is used to record every step of the process, providing transparency and ensuring that all data is immutable. This includes data on the farm, transportation, storage, and retail points. Each stakeholder (e.g., farmers, transporters, wholesalers, retailers) updates the blockchain with relevant information. The end result is a fully traceable food supply chain where the consumer can see exactly where and how their food was produced, transported, and stored.

Sample Data (Blockchain Tracking for Apples):

Step	Date	Location	Stakeholder	Action	Blockchain Entry
Harvest	2025-01-01	Farm A, USA	Farmer John	Apples harvested	Timestamp, Farmer ID, Quantity, Crop Type
Transport	2025-01-02	Warehouse B, USA	Trucking Co.	Transport to warehouse	Timestamp, Truck ID, Transport Time
Storage	2025-01-03	Warehouse B, USA	Warehouse Manager	Apples stored under proper conditions	Timestamp, Storage Temp, Quantity

Step	Date	Location	Stakeholder	Action	Blockchain Entry
Distribution	2025-01-04	Retailer C, USA	Distributor X	Delivered to retailer	Timestamp, Delivery Time, Quantity
Retail Sale	2025-01-05	Supermart D, USA	Retailer Y	Apples sold to customer	Timestamp, Customer ID, Quantity Sold

- Load the Data into a data analysis software / tool

- Analyze the data.

Output and Results in the Table:

- The blockchain records provide detailed, immutable, and transparent tracking of the apples from farm to consumer.

- All entries are time-stamped and verified by different stakeholders, ensuring no fraudulent activity or information tampering.

- Key data points include quantities, storage conditions, and specific transport times, which could be helpful in case of recalls or customer inquiries.

- The customer can view the apple's journey by scanning a QR code on the product's packaging.

Interpretation of Results:

- **Transparency**: The end-to-end transparency allows consumers to trust the food supply chain. They can see precisely when and where the apples were harvested, stored, and sold.

- **Efficiency**: If any issues arise (e.g., spoilage during storage), the precise data on storage conditions (e.g., temperature) can help trace the problem to its source quickly.

- **Traceability**: In case of a foodborne illness outbreak, the blockchain system can provide immediate access to the exact batch of apples involved, reducing the scope and cost of a recall.

Observations:

1. **Real-Time Access to Information**: Blockchain enables all stakeholders (including consumers) to access accurate, real-time information about the product's journey.

2. **Reduced Fraud and Counterfeiting**: The immutable nature of blockchain prevents data manipulation, ensuring that customers are getting what they paid for.

3. **Improved Responsiveness to Issues**: In case of issues like product recalls, the affected batches can be identified and isolated rapidly due to the transparent nature of the blockchain.

Decisions from the Supply Chain Management Perspective:

1. **Product Quality Control**: Supply chain managers can use blockchain data to monitor and enforce strict quality standards at every stage, especially in the transport and storage phases.

2. **Sustainability Decisions**: With transparency into farming practices (e.g., pesticide use or organic certification), companies can make decisions about which suppliers align with sustainability goals.

3. **Customer Confidence**: The ability to share detailed product journey data builds consumer trust and can be used as a selling point for marketing, especially in industries where ethical sourcing is a major concern.

By using blockchain for traceability and transparency, supply chain managers can not only improve operational efficiency but also enhance their brand's reputation, ensuring customers feel more secure and informed about the products they purchase.

12.2 The Role of Big Data and Cloud Computing

Big data and cloud computing have become pivotal in transforming how businesses, governments, and individuals operate in today's digital age. Big data refers to the massive volumes of structured and unstructured data generated from various sources, including social media, sensors, transactions, and more. This data is often too large and complex for traditional data-processing software to handle efficiently. Cloud computing, on the other hand, provides an online infrastructure that offers storage, processing power, and software services, enabling businesses and individuals to store and analyze large datasets without needing physical hardware or on-site IT teams.

The power of big data lies in its potential to unlock valuable insights and help organizations make more informed decisions. By analyzing vast amounts of data, companies can identify patterns, trends, and correlations that would have been difficult to detect manually. This ability to process and analyze data in real-time is particularly beneficial in industries such as healthcare, finance, retail, and marketing, where decisions often need to be made quickly and accurately.

Cloud computing facilitates big data analytics by providing the necessary resources on-demand. Instead of maintaining costly physical servers and infrastructure, businesses can rely on cloud platforms like Amazon Web Services (AWS), Microsoft Azure, or Google Cloud to scale their data storage and processing needs. This makes big data more accessible to companies of all sizes, from startups to large corporations, and enables them to tap into advanced analytics tools without heavy upfront investments.

The integration of big data and cloud computing also enhances collaboration and accessibility. Since cloud platforms are internet-based, they allow data and tools to be accessed from anywhere at any time. This facilitates better collaboration across departments, teams, or even organizations, regardless of geographical location. Furthermore, cloud computing can provide businesses with the flexibility to scale their operations quickly, responding to changes in demand or data growth without the need for major infrastructure changes.

One significant advantage of cloud computing in big data management is its cost-effectiveness. Traditionally, storing and processing large datasets required a considerable financial investment in IT infrastructure, software, and maintenance. With cloud solutions, businesses pay for what they use, meaning they only incur costs for the storage and processing power they need, making it a more efficient option. This "pay-as-you-go" model also allows organizations to experiment with big data without worrying about hefty upfront capital costs.

Lastly, the combination of big data and cloud computing is driving innovations in artificial intelligence (AI) and machine learning (ML). The massive datasets stored in the cloud provide the raw material needed to train sophisticated algorithms and predictive models. These models can then be used to improve everything from customer service chatbots to autonomous vehicles. As more data becomes available and cloud computing infrastructure continues to evolve, the potential for AI and ML to solve complex problems and create new opportunities continues to grow.

Practical Example: Leveraging Cloud Computing for Scalable Supply Chain Analytics in a Growing E-commerce Business

An e-commerce company has been expanding its operations, resulting in increased demand for supply chain optimization. To handle the growing data from inventory, order processing, shipping, and customer feedback, the company decides to migrate its supply chain analytics to the cloud. By leveraging cloud computing, the company can scale its data processing, run predictive analytics, and improve decision-making in real time.

Context: The company needs to analyze and optimize key performance indicators (KPIs) like inventory turnover, order fulfillment times, and customer satisfaction across multiple regions. Using cloud-based analytics tools, they integrate data from different systems (e.g., warehouse management, shipping logs, customer reviews) to produce real-time reports and forecasts. The results from cloud-based analytics help the company optimize stock levels, improve supplier relationships, and reduce order fulfillment delays.

Sample Data (Before Cloud Analytics Integration)

Product ID	Inventory Level	Order Fulfillment Time (days)	Customer Satisfaction Score	Supplier Lead Time (days)
P001	200	5	3.8	7
P002	150	7	4.2	9
P003	300	6	3.5	6
P004	100	8	4.0	10

Product ID	Inventory Level	Order Fulfillment Time (days)	Customer Satisfaction Score	Supplier Lead Time (days)
P005	250	4	4.5	5

- Load the Data into a data analysis software / tool

- Analyze the data.

Cloud Analytics Output (After Integration)

Product ID	Optimized Inventory Level	Predicted Order Fulfillment Time (days)	Predicted Customer Satisfaction Score	Optimized Supplier Lead Time (days)
P001	180	4	4.0	6
P002	140	6	4.1	8
P003	280	5	3.7	5
P004	120	7	4.2	9
P005	230	3	4.6	4

Explanation and Interpretation of Results:

- **Optimized Inventory Levels:** The cloud-based analytics tool provides insights into more efficient inventory levels by considering factors such as seasonality, order patterns, and supplier lead time. By reducing excess stock for high-turnover products (e.g., P001 and P002), the company can optimize warehouse space and reduce carrying costs.

- **Order Fulfillment Time:** The predictive analytics shows a reduction in fulfillment time for P001, P003, and P005. This improvement is likely due to better alignment of stock levels with demand and optimized routing in the distribution network. A more accurate forecast helps the company allocate resources more effectively, reducing delays.

- **Customer Satisfaction:** The analytics suggest a slight increase in customer satisfaction for most products (especially for P001 and P005). By improving stock availability and order fulfillment times, customer experience improves, as reflected in higher satisfaction scores.

- **Supplier Lead Time:** Cloud analytics help optimize supplier relationships by providing better visibility into lead times. For instance, P003's lead time is reduced from 6 days to 5 days by identifying more reliable suppliers or improving negotiation terms.

Observations:

1. **Reduced Stockouts:** With optimized inventory levels, the company avoids stockouts for fast-moving products (P005), improving overall customer satisfaction.

2. **Improved Fulfillment Efficiency:** Cloud-based predictive analytics leads to a better allocation of resources, resulting in faster fulfillment times.

3. **Cost Efficiency:** The optimized inventory helps reduce warehousing costs, and the company can focus on improving supplier performance by analyzing lead times in the cloud-based system.

4. **Data-Driven Decision Making:** Real-time analytics allows for timely adjustments in the supply chain, providing a significant competitive edge.

Supply Chain Management Decisions:

1. **Inventory Management:** Based on cloud analytics, reduce overstock for slower-moving products and increase stock for high-demand items.

2. **Supplier Optimization:** Renegotiate terms or find alternative suppliers for products like P002 (higher lead time), based on the data-driven insights.

3. **Logistics Efficiency:** Optimize fulfillment centers and shipping routes, especially for products like P005, to cut down on lead time and improve service delivery.

4. **Customer Experience Focus:** By analyzing customer satisfaction trends, focus efforts on improving order fulfillment for products

with low satisfaction scores (e.g., P003) by ensuring timely delivery and better packaging.

In conclusion, leveraging cloud computing for supply chain analytics allows e-commerce businesses to make data-driven decisions, improving efficiency, reducing costs, and enhancing customer satisfaction.

12.3 Future Prospects: Autonomous Supply Chains and AI Integration

As technology continues to advance, autonomous supply chains are becoming a promising vision for the future. These systems would use a combination of artificial intelligence, robotics, and the Internet of Things to manage and streamline logistics operations with minimal human intervention. With the power of AI, supply chains can automatically adjust to changes in demand, disruptions, or external factors such as weather, ensuring products reach consumers more efficiently and cost-effectively.

AI can revolutionize supply chain management by providing real-time data and predictive analytics. By processing vast amounts of information, AI can forecast trends, optimize inventory, and suggest the best routes for transportation. This allows businesses to reduce waste, lower costs, and meet customer demands more precisely. In turn, it improves the overall customer experience by reducing delays and enhancing product availability.

One of the key benefits of AI-powered autonomous supply chains is their ability to respond to disruptions. Whether it's a natural disaster, labor strike, or transportation bottleneck, AI systems can quickly re-route shipments, find alternative suppliers, or adjust production schedules. This flexibility ensures that the supply chain remains operational even under unforeseen circumstances, reducing the risk of product shortages and customer dissatisfaction.

Robotics is another integral part of these autonomous systems. Automated vehicles, drones, and robots can transport goods from warehouses to distribution centers or even directly to customers. These machines can operate 24/7, reducing the need for human labor while also cutting down on transportation costs. With the continued development of robotic technology, we could see the widespread adoption of fully autonomous delivery systems in the near future.

However, the integration of AI and automation into supply chains raises challenges, particularly around security and ethics. The reliance on technology for critical operations increases the risk of cyberattacks or system failures. Businesses will need to invest heavily in cybersecurity measures and ensure that AI decisions are transparent and accountable. Additionally, the shift toward automation may result in job displacement, requiring society to address issues like workforce retraining and equitable job opportunities.

Looking ahead, the future of autonomous supply chains holds great potential for both businesses and consumers. As AI technologies continue to evolve and become more sophisticated, supply chains will become increasingly efficient, resilient, and adaptive. The widespread adoption of these technologies promises a more streamlined global economy, where goods move faster, costs decrease, and the environmental impact of transportation and logistics is reduced. However, careful consideration of the social and ethical implications will be necessary to fully realize these benefits.

Practical Example: Exploring the Future of Autonomous Delivery Vehicles in Supply Chain Logistics

The adoption of autonomous delivery vehicles (ADVs) in supply chain logistics is gaining traction, with companies exploring their potential to reduce costs, improve delivery times, and enhance operational efficiency. In this practical example, we focus on a company that is testing autonomous electric delivery vehicles for last-mile deliveries in a metropolitan area. The company is evaluating the performance of these vehicles over a three-month period to assess key metrics such as cost per delivery, delivery time, and customer satisfaction. The results are compared against traditional delivery methods using human-driven vehicles.

Sample Data:

Month	Delivery Method	Total Deliveries	Total Cost (USD)	Total Time (hours)	Customer Satisfaction (1-10)
January	Traditional Vehicles	500	10,000	100	7
January	Autonomous Vehicles	500	8,000	80	8
February	Traditional Vehicles	520	10,400	105	7.2
February	Autonomous Vehicles	520	7,800	78	8.3
March	Traditional Vehicles	530	10,600	110	7.5

Month	Delivery Method	Total Deliveries	Total Cost (USD)	Total Time (hours)	Customer Satisfaction (1-10)
March	Autonomous Vehicles	530	7,900	75	8.5

- Load the Data into a data analysis software / tool
- Analyze the data.

Output and Results:

1. **Cost per Delivery**:
   - Traditional Vehicles: Total Cost / Total Deliveries
   - Autonomous Vehicles: Total Cost / Total Deliveries

Month	Traditional Vehicles Cost per Delivery (USD)	Autonomous Vehicles Cost per Delivery (USD)
January	20	16
February	20	15
March	20	14.91

2. **Average Delivery Time per Vehicle**:
   - Traditional Vehicles: Total Time / Total Deliveries
   - Autonomous Vehicles: Total Time / Total Deliveries

Month	Traditional Vehicles Time per Delivery (hours)	Autonomous Vehicles Time per Delivery (hours)
January	0.2	0.16
February	0.202	0.15
March	0.208	0.14

3. **Customer Satisfaction**:

  o Autonomous vehicles consistently outperform traditional
    methods with customer satisfaction scores above 8,
    compared to the traditional vehicle scores which remain
    around 7.5.

Interpretation of Results:

- **Cost Savings**: Autonomous vehicles show a steady reduction in cost
  per delivery over the three-month period, with costs falling from $16
  to $14.91 per delivery, while traditional vehicles maintain a steady
  cost of $20 per delivery. This demonstrates the potential for
  significant cost savings when switching to autonomous delivery
  systems.

- **Time Efficiency**: Autonomous vehicles also reduce delivery time,
  with a decrease in time per delivery from 0.16 hours to 0.14 hours,
  suggesting a 12.5% reduction in time spent per delivery. Traditional
  vehicles show a marginal increase in time spent per delivery over
  the same period.

- **Customer Satisfaction**: Autonomous vehicles also show a slight
  improvement in customer satisfaction, with scores rising from 8 to
  8.5. This could be attributed to faster deliveries, fewer errors, and
  the novelty of the service.

Observations:

1. **Cost and Time Efficiency**: Autonomous vehicles are proving to be
   more cost-effective and time-efficient compared to traditional
   methods. Over time, the difference in both metrics will likely
   increase as autonomous vehicles become more optimized.

2. **Customer Experience**: Customer satisfaction is higher with
   autonomous vehicles, which may be due to their ability to provide
   more reliable, timely deliveries. This could improve customer
   loyalty and brand reputation.

3. **Scalability**: As the company continues to scale the use of
   autonomous vehicles, the cost advantages should become more
   pronounced, leading to greater profitability.

Decisions from a Supply Chain Management Perspective:

1. **Investment in Autonomous Vehicles**: Given the observed cost and
   time savings, as well as the positive impact on customer satisfaction,
   the company should consider expanding its fleet of autonomous

vehicles. Long-term investments in this technology could yield even greater efficiencies.

2. **Optimization of Delivery Routes**: The company should invest in advanced routing algorithms for the autonomous vehicles to further optimize delivery times and reduce costs. This could include dynamic route adjustments based on real-time traffic data.

3. **Monitor Customer Satisfaction**: As autonomous vehicles become more integrated into the delivery network, customer feedback should be closely monitored to ensure that satisfaction remains high. The company could also explore offering premium services, such as autonomous vehicle deliveries for urgent or high-priority shipments.

4. **Risk Assessment**: While the autonomous vehicles provide many advantages, there is a need for a risk mitigation strategy related to potential technological failures, regulatory changes, and public acceptance of autonomous vehicles.

By closely monitoring these metrics and scaling their use of autonomous delivery vehicles, companies can gain a competitive edge in the rapidly evolving logistics landscape.

www.ingramcontent.com/pod-product-compliance
Lightning Source LLC
LaVergne TN
LVHW081523050326
832903LV00025B/1604